RAILWAYS OF CANADA

by
ROBERT F. LEGGET

DOUGLAS & McINTYRE: VANCOUVER

Douglas & McIntyre Ltd.
1615 Venables Street
Vancouver, British Columbia

First published in hardback by David & Charles
(Holdings) Limited, South Devon House, Newton
Abbot, Devon, England

Canadian Cataloguing in Publication Data

Legget, Robert F., 1904-
    Railways of Canada

    Previously published under title: Railroads of
Canada.
    Bibliography: p.
    Includes index.
    ISBN 0-88894-269-9 pa.

    1. Railroads - Canada - History.   I. Title.
II. Title: Railroads of Canada.
HE2808.L43 1980   385'.0971   C80-091116-4

Printed and bound in Canada

Contents

6 *Contents*

List of Illustrations

LIST OF MAPS

William Cobbett, in 1825, 'was convinced that the *facilities* which now exist of *moving human bodies from place to place*, are amongst the *curses* of the country, the destroyers of industry, of morals, and, of course, of happiness' (and the italics are his). —From *Rural Rides*, Penguin English Library, London 1967, p 292.

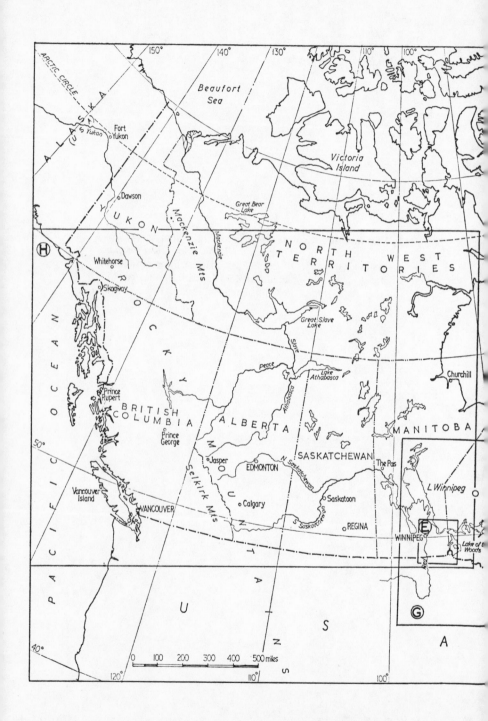

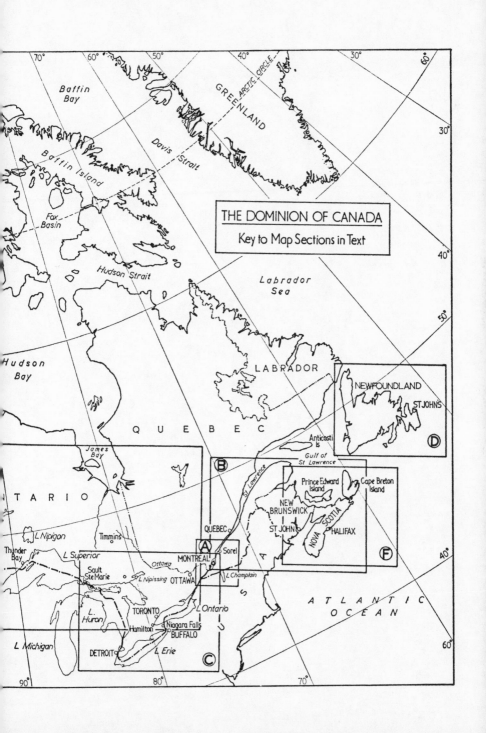

THE DOMINION OF CANADA
Key to Map Sections in Text

Introduction

'Inasmuch as the Provinces of Canada, Nova Scotia, and New Brunswick has joined in a Declaration that the construction of the Intercolonial Railway is essential to the Consolidation of the Union of British North America. . . .' These are the opening words of Section 145 of the British North America Act, passed by the British Parliament in the early months of 1867 and proclaimed in Ottawa on 1 July of that year. It established the Dominion of Canada. It remains, with some modifications, the written constitution of the modern independent Canadian nation. It may well be the only written national constitution that specifically links the construction of a major railway with the establishment of a new country, but in this it accurately reflects the vital part that railways played in early Canada. They still do today.

Canada is the second largest country in the world, its area of almost four million square miles exceeded only by that of the USSR. From Halifax on the Atlantic coast to Victoria on the Pacific is three hundred miles further than the distance by air from Halifax across the Atlantic to Prestwick in Scotland. A journey sometimes taken by the writer from his office in Ottawa (already a thousand miles from the open sea) to the town of Inuvik on the Arctic coast is slightly longer than the journey eastward from Ottawa through Montreal to London, England, and there are still the Arctic islands of the Queen Elizabeth archipelago to traverse before the limits of Canada are reached. It is not surprising, therefore, to find that from the far south of Canada to its northern tip is about as far as from Montreal to Vancouver, from sea to sea. And the southern tip at Point Pelee on Lake Erie, is well to the south of the northern border of California.

In so vast a land transportation has always been, and will always be the key to its development and well-being. The canoe journeys of the Canadian pioneers were often epic journeys, distances of one hundred miles in a day being not uncommon, but they carried only a few hundreds along the waterways. Distances are such that the early roads were merely links between water routes, and it was not until the coming of the railways that any major settlement could proceed other than on the banks of rivers and lakes. How the early railways penetrated the forests, the plains and the mountains of Canada will be a part of the story related in the pages that follow. Today, railways are giving good service in all ten provinces, in the Yukon Territory and even in the North-west Territories. Their passenger services have been seriously curtailed due to the inroads of automobile and air transport, just as has been the case in so many other countries, but they still carry passengers and, in the case of small settlements still not served by roads, provide the only normal access to the outside world.

Distance was the main difficulty in building the early railways, the terrain of eastern Canada containing no high mountains although much hilly country. This necessitated great skill in location, the wonder of aerial surveying being still something for the future. Tunnels on Canadian railways are therefore few but bridges are many, the size of even secondary rivers being such that many long bridges on even secondary rail lines were essential. The Ottawa River, for example, is only a tributary of the St Lawrence and yet its average flow is greater than the average flow of all the rivers of the United Kingdom. It is not surprising that the first railway bridge across it was not built until 1880 and that the second, when built in 1900, was the longest steel cantilever bridge in North America. The Quebec Bridge and the Victoria Bridge in Montreal, the latter notable in being built as early as 1860, are world renowned.

The great mountain barrier of the far west presented a real obstacle to transcontinental rail connection but it was finally overcome first by the building of the Canadian Pacific Railway

(CPR) in the 1880s. It may surprise some readers to find that the building of the CPR does not receive attention until more than a third of the way through this book, but this is an accurate reflection of its place in Canadian railway history—a splendid achievement but only one part of an epic story, the foundations of which were well and truly laid several decades before the dream of the transcontinental railway was first realised.

Climate provides a peculiarly Canadian problem for railway operation as well as for railway building. Temperatures throughout most of the country have an unusual range, from 30° below zero C to 30° above being annually experienced throughout most of Canada, Vancouver Island always excepted. On the prairies and in colder parts of Ontario and Quebec, winter temperatures can drop as low as 50° below zero C, while summer temperatures frequently go above 33°. Winds and rain are not unusual, except for the high rainfall on the west coast due to the Coast Range Mountains, but snow provides an almost unique operating problem. Falls totalling over 30 ft of snow in one winter are not unusual in the mountains, depths of snow on the ground often being higher than single-storey buildings. Even in Ottawa, the nation's capital city, the winter of 1970–71 saw a record total snowfall of almost 15 ft. There were those who, in the early days of Canadian railroading, said that some lines would have to close down during the winter but this has never been necessary. Snow-fighting and snow-clearing have been developed to a most efficient degree on all Canadian railways, but the fact that such conditions do have to be faced will explain the unusually 'heavy' appearance of railroad rolling stock.

Despite all these problems, the railroads of Canada have been developed into a splendid transportation system, now with a total mileage of over 40,000 miles, most of it in single-track lines. At one time, this represented one mile of track for every three hundred people. Today, with rising population and little change in mileage, it still represents only 500 people per mile of track compared with about 800 in the United States and over 2,600 in the United Kingdom. The economic burden that the railways represent in Canada is but one of the consequences of its vast size. It is an essential burden but it has created some built-in financial problems with which successive governments have had to deal.

The total mileage is divided between about two dozen railways, all but two relatively small lines. The Canadian Pacific Railway (CPR) accounts for rather more than one-third of the total and Canadian National Railways (CNR)—the 'largest railway system in North America'—well over one-half. The existence of these two great railways side by side, usually competing but often co-operating—the one wholly owned by the people of Canada through the medium of a special Crown company, the other one of the world's great private-enterprise corporations, owned by its stockholders, the vast majority of whom today are Canadians—this surprising situation is the constant mystery facing visitors to Canada who are interested in railways, and especially those from the United States. How this unusual, even Gilbertian, situation arose, how the railways of Canada grew out of small portage links, how they are operated today, and what their prospects are for the future, it is the purpose of this book to describe.

Page 17. (Above) *Canada's oldest locomotive, 'Samson', built at Newcastle-on-Tyne by Timothy Hackworth in 1838 and now on show in New Glasgow, Nova Scotia;* (below) *the Carillon portage train of the Carillon & Grenville Railway, a photograph taken near the end of the nineteenth century*

Page 18. *A 100-ton Mountain engine heads a special train carrying an inspection party on the newly completed Canadian Pacific Railway in 1889*

CHAPTER 1

The Beginnings 1836-54

British North America, at the start of the railway era, consisted of five small and struggling colonies clustered around the Gulf and River St Lawrence. Newfoundland, a separate colony at the mouth of the great Gulf, then and for well over a century more was proud of her independence from 'the mainland'. Down by the sea Nova Scotia (but recently joined by Cape Breton Island), New Brunswick and Prince Edward Island, each had its own lieutenant-governor and separate administration. Along the shores of the River St Lawrence, Lower Canada was still working out the best form of liaison between French-speaking and English-speaking residents, following the transfer of power in 1763, a process not yet fully completed. And up on the wooded shores of Lake Ontario and beyond, a few small new settlements were banded together as Upper Canada, separated from what was to become the province of Quebec only in 1792. It would not be until 1867, as a result of the passage of the British North America Act, that these diverse political units would be united into a federation that was then so happily called the Dominion of Canada, the beginning of the nation of Canada of today.

In those early days, practically all pioneer settlements were located on waterways, travel being almost entirely by water when navigation was possible, and by sleigh over the snow and ice of winter. Quebec City had been the first major settlement, with its commanding position near the end of tidal water in the St Lawrence. Montreal had followed, located on its island site by the existence of the great Lachine Rapids, the first real impediment to travel by boat up the great river. York, as Toronto was originally named, was still a tiny village located at the mouths of the Don and Humber rivers, an important starting point for the long portage from Lake Ontario to Lake Simcoe and so into Lake Huron. Indicative of the early stage of development of the group of colonies were the populations of these three major cities of today in the year 1825, the year in which the Bill authorising the Liverpool to Manchester Railway was finally passed. Quebec had a population of 22,101; Montreal had only just passed this figure with 22,357; York had only 1,677, whereas today Toronto and its environs exceeds the two million mark, second only to Montreal among the cities of Canada, both of them now numbered among the major cities of the world.

Small wonder, therefore, that it was to be some years before the advantages of rail travel were to be recognised in Canada, even though steamboats were introduced on the St Lawrence River as early as 1809 (using a Boulton & Watt engine) and on the Ottawa River in 1820. This initiative in improving water travel was in keeping with the vital importance of journeys by water in the life of the colonies. There were a few routes upon which ran a number of stage-coach services, but the roads were poor and the distances such that there was little to choose between the discomforts and delays of coach travel and the inconvenience of travel by water, with the necessary disembarking, walking and embarking again at every portage that was encountered. *Portage* used in this way betrays by its French origin its traditional usage by French Canadian *voyageurs* as they explored under inspired leaders the continent of North America starting from their homes on the St Lawrence, using the Ottawa and Mattawa rivers as the gateway to the Great Lakes and so to the Arctic, the far West, the Great Plains and the Mississippi River and its tributaries.

It was a natural and logical development that railways should have been first thought of in Canada as a substitute for portage transport of the accustomed kind, goods carried on simple carts, or more usually on men's backs. But the first public steam-operated railway in Canada effected a portage of a different kind, a great reduction in the length of one of the important travel routes of the time by what was a very long portage in the ordinary sense but a relatively short railway line when it was completed. All traffic between Montreal and Lower Canada in general, and New York and the coastal settlements of the United States, was by boat along the Hudson River, through Lake Champlain and so into the Richelieu River of Canada which joins the St Lawrence at Sorel. Once in the St Lawrence, vessels had to sail forty miles up the St Lawrence to Montreal, whereas the nearest point on the Richelieu to Montreal, across land, was only fourteen and a half miles away. This short cut was between the small settlement of St Johns (originally Dorchester) on the Richelieu and La Prairie on the south shore of the St Lawrence immediately opposite Montreal. Since St Johns is just over fifty miles from the mouth of the Richelieu River, this 'short-cut' obviated over ninety miles of river travel. St Johns, therefore, early became a settlement of importance, the pivotal point in the transportation system of the Champlain Transportation Co which provided the river service to New York. It was an enterprising merchant of St Johns, Jason C. Pierce, who was the prime mover in the final organisation of the Champlain & St Lawrence Railroad.

An Act authorising the new railway had been passed by the Legislature of Lower Canada in 1832, but it required the enthusiasm of Pierce and his fellow directors to assemble enough capital for the relatively simple construction job. The terrain traversed by the line was reasonably flat, two gradients only being necessary and three curves. One long but low embankment had to be constructed, four small bridges over streams and one major bridge over the Little River (Rivière l'Acadie) which was 400 ft long. It is still possible to trace on foot the remains of the roadbed of this pioneer Canadian line, and even today, part of the route is followed by a CNR main line to the south.

The first locomotive engine for rail service in Canada was

ordered from Robert Stephenson & Co, then of Newcastle-on-Tyne. The order was booked by them on 26 October 1835, the engine being the 127th which they had built. It was one of the 'Samson' type already standardised by these builders, with 0—4—0 wheel arrangement. With 9 × 14 in cylinders and 48 in diameter wooden wheels, the engine weighed 12,563 lb in working order. Its wheelbase was only 5 ft and so it proved to be unsteady if operated at any but low speeds. It was named *Dorchester*, in honour of the name carried by the town of St Johns from 1815 to 1835. Despite difficulties, it did operate the first railway train in Canada on Thursday, 21 July 1836, pulling two coaches from La Prairie to St Johns and back at an average speed of 14.5 mph in the presence of the Governor-General, Lord Gosford. The railway history of Canada had started.

The new service made a slow and uncertain start, the political uprising of 1837 interfering somewhat with regular operation. The infant railway was rented by the military authorities for two weeks in 1838. By 1839, however, good dividends were being paid to the shareholders, and two new Norris locomotives had been purchased. Such was the progress made that the original locomotive had its wheel arrangement altered from 0—4—0 to 4—2—0 to give better riding characteristics. In this form it served until the late forties when it was replaced by a Norris and a Baldwin, both 4—4—0s, and by a new engine built at Dundee in Scotland. This was called the *John Molson* which, although thought to have been built as a 2—2—2, was later rebuilt as a 4—2—2. In this form it served until about 1874, in which year it is believed to have been cut up. Records of its appearance survived, fortunately, and were used by the Canadian Railroad Historical Association (CRHA) in having a full-scale working replica made in 1971 (in Japan!) for display and use in the Association's museum near Montreal. It is therefore possible to see today what one of the very earliest Canadian locomotives looked like, even though all that has remained of the *Dorchester* is one of its nameplates, now a valued relic in the museum of Joliette College.

Joliette is today a busy town about thirty miles to the north of the centre of Montreal and twelve miles from the River St Lawrence. It achieved fame early in railroad history since it was the terminus of the third Canadian railway. This was built in 1849–50 by La Compagnie du Chemin à Rails du Saint-Laurent et du village d'Industrie, a twelve-mile-long line from what is now Lanorai on the great river to the fledgling industrial centre. The Champlain & St Lawrence Co were able to dispose of two of their first stud of three locomotives to this new line, and to do so profitably. The *Dorchester* served until 1864 when it was damaged in an accident; the *Jason C. Pierce* (as the second locomotive had been named), having been rebuilt as a 4—4—0, remained in service until about 1886, a remarkable record for so early an engine. Pierce himself died on 4 September 1851, and only in recent years has his contribution to Canadian railroading been generally appreciated.

The great canoe routes from Montreal to the West all had to start at the village of Lachine, a small settlement on Lake St Louis, nine miles to the west of the city. The lake is an enlarged portion of the River St Lawrence with a drop of 46 ft between its smooth waters and the harbour of Montreal. This drop was, and still is, taken up by the fall in the majestic Lachine Rapids, the existence of which led to the founding of Montreal at the head of river navigation from the sea. A portage around the Lachine Rapids was therefore the key to all travel to the West and North. One of the earliest coach services in Canada used the trail that had been formed by the steady succession of travellers along this portage since the early 1600s. An attempt to build a by-pass canal was made as early as 1680 but it was not until 1825 that the first commercially-usable canal around the Rapids was opened for service. So vital was this portage route that it is not surprising that the idea of building a railway to supplement the canal followed very closely upon the successful initiation of the railway from La Prairie to St Johns.

James Ferrier, the first of the many Scots Canadians to

contribute to Canada's railway history, decided in 1844 to promote the idea of a Lachine railway. The enabling Act was passed on 9 June 1846. Alexander Millar, an engineer brought over from Scotland to build the line, laid out a direct route from a terminus on Chaboliez Square in Montreal to a wharf at Lachine, roughly parallel with the canal, and eight miles long. Construction was impeded by a large bog (a parallel with Chat Moss) but eventually construction was complete. The first train, again honoured by the presence of the Governor-General, Lord Elgin, travelled from Montreal to Lachine on Friday, 19 November 1847, at a speed of 25 mph. Activities were discontinued for the winter but operations were resumed in earnest in the spring of 1848 and soon a service of six round trips a day was being operated. Local traffic was carried from the start to five stops intermediate between Montreal and Lachine, so that the Montreal & Lachine Rail Road (MLRR)

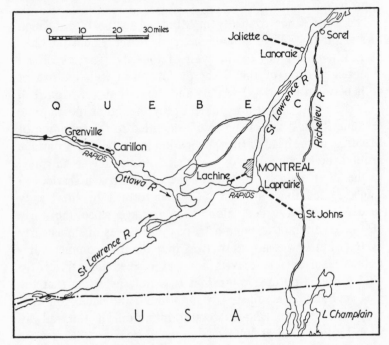

Map A: The first railways in Canada

can be said to have provided Canada's first suburban train service.

Its main traffic, however, was to the wharf at Lachine and gradually this became a busy point of transhipment. The MLRR was, therefore, a true 'portage railway' and it continued to serve in this way until as late as 1910. Until that year, and throughout each summer navigation season, a special train left Bonaventure Station (usually at 0800 hr) carrying passengers who transferred at Lachine Wharf to the graceful white river steamer that would convey them to Carillon on the Lake of Two Mountains, the terminus of the first part of the day-long river journey to Ottawa, the nation's capital city, 120 miles away. These special trains were, however, Grand Trunk trains, for the little line was taken over by the Grand Trunk interests as early as 1863, becoming the first short link in the main line from Montreal to Toronto. The wharf at Lachine still stands, although not now used by railway traffic. The route of the original portage line, however, is still in use as the first section of what is now the main line of CNR.

A quick glance at the map on p 40 is now necessary. On this will be seen the great water route to the West provided by the Ottawa and Mattawa rivers. This was first seen by Champlain in 1615 and thereafter used for over two hundred years by the explorers, missionaries, fur-traders and travellers who were ready to undertake the rigours of this 440-mile canoe journey to Lake Huron with its forty-seven portages around rapids— a route of great scenic beauty but treacherous indeed for the unwary *voyageur*. Between Lachine and Ottawa there were only two such stretches of rough water, a small rapids at Ste Anne de Bellevue, circumvented by successively larger single locks from the year 1816; and the Long Sault and Carillon Rapids, constituting a ten-mile stretch of very rough water starting at the head of the Lake of Two Mountains. The British Government built three small canals around these rapids between 1819 and 1834, as a military precaution, but they were naturally used for civilian traffic from the start. Passage through their eleven locks was a slow and tedious business, however, and so before long another portage railway was constructed to supplement the canals.

First proposed in 1840, the Carillon & Grenville Railway was not constructed until 1854; it continued in regular operation until the cessation in 1910 of the scheduled steamboat service between Montreal and Ottawa. It was the only section built of a grandiose scheme for a railway to be called the 'Great Montreal & Ottawa Valley Trunk Line', the detailed story of which is one of the almost unbelievable romances of Canadian railroading. Although part of the route of the little 12½-mile line is now followed by a CNR branch line, the Carillon & Grenville Railway itself remained throughout its lifetime quite isolated from the rest of the Canadian railroad system—and so retained its original broad gauge, as will later be related. Its single locomotive and two coaches served as the 'portage train', so well known to the many travellers on the Ottawa River route that was such an attractive means of travel to and from Canada's capital for well over half a century. The little train would be waiting, with steam up, when the morning boat from Montreal arrived. Trans-shipment was expeditious. Twenty minutes were required for the journey up the line to Grenville where the companion vessel which had sailed down the sixty miles from Ottawa that morning would be waiting to receive the passengers, ready to sail upstream again to Ottawa as soon as the last transfer had been made. (Picture, p 17.)

This happy combination of railroad and steamship services has been a special feature of railway development in Canada. As recently as the early 1960s, CPR still operated special trains from Toronto to Port McNicol, throughout the navigation season, connecting with its own fine passenger steamers that sailed as far west as Thunder Bay at the head of Lake Superior. The early days of railway progress in Canada presented this peculiar Canadian feature in a variety of ways. On the Ottawa River, for example, the first rapid above the Chaudière Rapids at Ottawa was a magnificent, turbulent waterfall known as Chats Falls. Here, too, a portage railway was built, three miles in length, on the north side of the great river. A prominent engineer once said that it 'had been designed out of the *Encyclopaedia Britannica*' since it had no grades, even at the expense of building some high wooden trestles. This was just as well, however, since its two small passenger cars were hauled by a white horse, again operated in connection with the upstream and downstream sailings of scheduled river steamers. Opened in 1846 (and so one of the pioneer Canadian lines), built to a 3-ft gauge, it operated its simple service until regular riverboat passenger traffic was peremptorily terminated on this section of the Ottawa in 1879.

At the famous confluence with the Mattawa River, the Ottawa turns north and very quickly assumes a turbulent character, there being several notable rapids before the smooth waters of Lake Temiskaming are reached. Here, too, a narrow-gauge portage railway was built near the end of the century under the inspired leadership of a pioneer missionary priest to hasten the settlement of what was then the wild, untouched forested areas adjacent to the river. It was later absorbed into a CPR branchline that is still in operation for freight service. Between the larger lakes in this well-wooded part of Ontario, small railways were built to replace the portage trails along which freight had previously been laboriously moved on men's backs. One of the most recent of these, constructed in 1900 between Peninsula Lake and Lake of Bays in the Huntsville district, came to be known as 'the shortest railway in the world', being only one and one-eighth of a mile long. Built to a gauge of 3 ft 6 in, it was steam-operated, and provided a regular (and most useful) service until the early sixties.

One of the yet-untold parts of the Canadian railway story is the way in which small railways have assisted travellers in the more remote parts of the vast country. Naturally located on the traditional river and canoe routes, these small lines must have been constructed with extraordinary difficulty for some of them had steel (or iron) rails, all of which would have had to be brought in by canoe, so remote were their locations. One of the earliest was the $4\frac{1}{4}$-mile line built to circumvent the Grand

Rapids of the Saskatchewan River that had to be faced by all travellers to the West as they left Lake Winnipeg to use either one or other of the two branches of this great river of the prairies. Far more remote was the mile-long line built at some date unknown in the early nineteenth century around the Robinson Portage, on the Hayes River, part of the canoe route from York Factory on Hudson Bay to Lake Winnipeg. Some of its iron-plated rails were found intact in 1956 by some modern *voyageurs*. They found also the rusted remains of a flat car large enough to convey a York boat or its load. Farther to the west, a half-mile narrow-gauge line had been constructed to bypass the Grand Rapids on the Athabasca River; this was in active use as late as 1911.

Early travellers on the rivers of Canada were naturally attracted by the virgin forests to be seen on either side of their canoe routes. Some settled at strategic points on river banks and proceeded to cut down their trees, mainly to clear their land but sometimes to sell the valuable timber thus procured. The Ottawa River valley was one of the first major areas to be the scene of lumbering on a large scale, initially for long spars of white pine for the British Navy, but for heavy timbers and sawn lumber after the first third of the nineteenth century. By mid-century a healthy trade in lumber with the United States had developed. Initially, shipments were made down the Ottawa River and the canals that had been built in connection with it, but once railways came to be accepted they offered the prospect of faster shipments for this increasingly important export. One of the first railways to be built in Canada for reasons other than to provide passage along a portage was planned to connect the fledgling lumber mills at what is now Ottawa (then named Bytown) directly with the US market.

One of the first railroads in the north-eastern part of the United States was yet another super-portage railway, between Ogdensburgh on the St Lawrence River and the head of Lake Champlain. It thus connected the end point of navigation on Lake Ontario with the great water route between New York and the St Lawrence, already mentioned. The first train steamed into Ogdensburgh on 20 September 1850. One of the engineers for this pioneer line was Walter Shanley, one of two Canadian brothers who, in those early days, became famous indeed as civil engineers of note. In later years, they were called in to complete the five-mile long Hoosac Tunnel through the Berkshires in Massachusetts, still the longest railroad tunnel east of the Mississippi.

The small Canadian town of Prescott faced Ogdensburgh across the St Lawrence, here only about a mile wide, and it was an obvious next step to build a railway from the nearest point on the Ottawa River so that lumber could be sent down this line, across the river at Prescott, and so on to the cars of the Ogdensburgh & Lake Champlain Railroad for shipment to the many settlements served by this line in northern New York State, or all the way to Lake Champlain for transhipment to boat for the journey down to the growing markets around New York. A group of enthusiastic citizens of Bytown therefore organised the Bytown & Prescott Railway Co (the name had to be changed to Ottawa & Prescott after Bytown acquired its new name in 1855). Its charter was granted on 10 August 1850. Walter Shanley was engaged as the engineer, somewhat reluctantly on his part, but had soon laid out what he thought to be a very good location across the relatively level country between the two great rivers. The first sod was turned in September 1851 and construction of this significant 57-mile long railway then began.

Although the necessary engineering works were not heavy, the line had to be built through country much of which was still virgin bush. Progress was not fast; the usual difficulties that seemed to surround the building of all these early lines plagued the owners in good measure. In the face of rapidly growing impatience in Bytown and much vocal opposition, the initial supply of 54,000 tons of iron rails, purchased in May 1853 in South Wales, ran out a few miles south of Bytown. Robert Bell, the energetic promoter of the line, was dismayed but not defeated, and for these last few miles from Billings into Rideau Falls on the Ottawa, he had wooden rails laid.

These were capped with iron straps, and on this makeshift track the first train steamed into Bytown late in the afternoon of Christmas Day 1854. Passengers had to be ferried across the Rideau River in order to reach the small settlement of Bytown, the necessary bridge not being constructed until later, but the line was complete and regular traffic began early in 1855. Financial troubles were serious from the start, the promoters' hopes being over-optimistic. The depression of 1857 did not help, nor did the claims for payment by the Ebbw Vale Iron Co of London, England, who had supplied the iron rails. The fledgling company had to be placed in receivership in 1858, a situation which lasted for seven years. Then followed two years of disuse until a new company, the Saint Lawrence & Ottawa Railway Co, was organised and took over the line on 21 December 1867. Service has been continuous since then, for this was one of the many local lines taken over by the CPR towards the end of the century.

As in other countries, there must have been some small tram railways in operation even before the late 1830s in different parts of British North America. There were almost certainly some in use between the quarries opened up to provide stone for the masonry of the locks on the Rideau Canal, between Bytown and Kingston. There is some record of an inclined tramway, operated as a funicular with two tracks, leading from wharves at Quebec City up to the Citadel and used for conveying stone for the building of this great fortress. It appears to have been operated by a simple steam engine at the foot as early as 1830.

Down in Canada's Maritime Provinces coalmines were being developed in Nova Scotia, some of the earliest around the small port of Pictou. As early as 1818 a small tramway was built from the wharves to coalmines on the East River but haulage was by horses. In 1838, however, three locomotives arrived from England. Built at Newcastle-on-Tyne, they were unusual Hackworth machines with 0—6—0 wheel arrangement, vertical cylinders and an old hook-type of motion, the fireman standing on a platform in the front of the engine. *Samson* was the name of the first, and it operated between the Frood mine and Pictou wharf. With its sister engine the *Albion*, it was taken to the World's Fair in Chicago in 1893 as one of the railroad historical exhibits, travelling on a flat car from Truro, Nova Scotia. It was preserved following its return to Canada and is now housed in a small building on Archimedes Street, New Glasgow, Nova Scotia. (Picture, p 17.) Here, within a few yards of the waters of the Atlantic, interested visitors can see one of the original locomotives of Canada and so be reminded of the progress made in railway motive power in the hundred and thirty-four years since the *Samson* was first greeted at Pictou by one of the greatest Highland parties that Nova Scotia has ever seen.

CHAPTER 2

The Grand Trunk: 1845-62

These were the beginnings, slow and halting but audacious in their day. When it is remembered that travellers to the West were still journeying up the Ottawa River by canoe long after the first trains ran in Canada, then the vision of the early builders will be better appreciated. The times were unsettled politically; the uprisings of 1837 in both Lower and Upper Canada had left an unfortunate legacy. The enquiry of Lord Durham, and the subsequent linking of the two political units into the combined Province of Canada in 1841, assisted in the development of the young country but still left some major problems unsolved, problems that led eventually to the Confederation of 1867. It is not too surprising, therefore, that by 1850, only sixty-eight miles of railway were in actual operation in British North America, although a number of other lines were in the planning stage. This limited progress may be compared with the 6,621 miles already in operation in Great Britain, and the 9,021 miles already completed and in use in the United States. The rapid advance in railway construction being achieved by her neighbour to the south led Canada to accelerate her own activity in this field, and the 1850s saw the start of the major pattern of rail connections in eastern Canada, culminating in 1860 in the opening of the great Victoria Bridge across the River St Lawrence at Montreal.

There had naturally been disappointments, especially in the Maritime Provinces, then the colonies of Nova Scotia and New Brunswick. They had close ties with Great Britain and for this reason, perhaps, were the first parts of Canada to catch the 'railway fever' that was so interesting a feature of much of the early railway promotion in Canada as elsewhere. In Nova Scotia there were railroad visionaries but, somewhat surprisingly, it was in the younger province of New Brunswick that action began. The small settlements of Saint John (at the mouth of the Saint John River, on the Bay of Fundy) and Saint Andrews (on Passamaquoddy Bay, fifty miles south of Saint John) were competing with each other as potential ocean terminals. Saint John was the ultimate winner but it was from Saint Andrews (today a small quiet town) that the first major railroad of Canada was proposed, a line connecting Saint Andrews-by-the-Sea (as it has been known) with Quebec City, 250 miles away. A serious proposal for such a line was published in the *United Service Journal* for 1832; after an initial survey had been started, a 'Saint Andrews & Quebec Rail Road Association' was formed in Saint Andrews; and both a charter and a subsidy from the British Government were obtained in 1836. Unfortunately, the proposed line ran through Maine, then disputed territory under study by a joint British-American commission, and at the request of the American Government all work was stopped. By the Webster-Ashburton Treaty (one of Britain's most unfortunate legacies to Canada) most of the surveyed land became US territory and so the whole scheme had temporarily to be abandoned. Ground was finally broken at Saint Andrews only in 1847 and construction optimistically started, but it was to be twenty years more before the little line even reached Woodstock, seventy-five miles away, by which time the company was bankrupt.

There were other even more grandiose schemes afoot. In Halifax, two alternative routes to the colonies of Canada were proposed, the Halifax & Quebec, and the European & North American railways. The latter was one of the first of the many grandiloquent titles with which early Canadian lines were to be blessed. They were used in all seriousness but some now appear to be so absurd that an apology for their inclusion in this volume almost seems called for. But they must be used, indicative as they are of the great possibilities that railroads appeared to present in those pioneer days. Both proposals anticipated a line crossing Nova Scotia by approximately the same route, to the isthmus of Chignecto where it would enter New Brunswick. Thence alternative routes were planned, one generally along the north shore of the province to Quebec City and the other to Montreal through Maine.

A committee was formed in 1844 in London, England, for the purpose of building the former line. Meetings were held in Halifax and Saint John with much enthusiasm, and the route chosen by the surveyor, Major Robinson, was the one that was later used by the Intercolonial Railway. The provinces all supported the idea and offered generous grants and subsidies but the British Government would advance no help. Joseph Howe, a great political leader of the time, was sent to London from Nova Scotia to reopen the matter, and eventually an agreement was reached. The Government of Canada passed legislation authorising the aid they would give but then misunderstandings developed, great bitterness was generated and the entire scheme collapsed, not to be resurrected until the time of Confederation.

Joseph Howe became one of the railway commissioners of Nova Scotia, under whose auspices a line was built from Halifax to Truro with a branch to Windsor between 1854 and 1858, the line being extended to Pictou by 1867. In New Brunswick, in addition to the line that eventually reached Woodstock, another was built in 1860 from Saint John to Shediac on the northern coast. By the time of Confederation there were, therefore, 145 miles of railway in Nova Scotia and 226 miles in New Brunswick. Small though these totals were, the lines built included some critical transportation links, as the map will show, connecting the Atlantic with the Bay of Fundy, and both with the Gulf of St Lawrence. All the lines mentioned are still in use, that from Halifax to Truro being now a part of the vitally important CNR main line to the sea.

Page 35. (Above) *Snow plough operated by four wood-burning locomotives at Chaudière Junction, Quebec, on the Grand Trunk Railways in the 1890s; (below) an early train ferry on the Canada Atlantic Railway at Coteau Landing, Quebec, for conveying* CAR *trains from its main line up the Ottawa Valley across the river St Lawrence to its extension to the US border; about 1890*

Page 36. *Great Western Railway train crossing the original Suspension Bridge at Niagara Falls linking Canada with the United States*

With some links to the ill-fated European & North American proposal, discussions had begun early in the forties about the possibility of linking Montreal with the closest point on the Atlantic coast at Portland, Maine. Montrealers did not get excited about this prospect, although the citizens of the intermediate Canadian town of Sherbrooke did set up a supporting committee in 1843. In 1845 there was initiated a bonding system for the transfer of goods across the Canadian-US boundary and this immediately changed the prospects for this projected line. A young lawyer from Portland, John A. Poor, saw how his city could be the ice-free winter port for Montreal, winter navigation on the St Lawrence being then unthought of, and it was due to his enthusiasm that this important line was constructed. Two companies were incorporated in 1845, the Atlantic & St Lawrence (AStLR) for the US section, and the St Lawrence & Atlantic (StLAR) for the Canadian. As no financial assistance was forthcoming from the Government of Canada, all its available funds having been designated for canal construction, A. T. Galt was sent to England to try to raise the necessary capital. The first of a succession of Canadian financiers who were to make this suppliant's journey, Galt was successful but, unfortunately, the market collapse of 1845 intervened before full payments on the bonds he had sold could be collected. Failure seemed inevitable.

The directors again appealed to the Canadian Government with the result that, in 1849, there was passed the first of a succession of major pieces of legislation regarding the construction of railways, the Guarantee Act. This guaranteed interest at 6 per cent on not more than half the bonds for any railway more than seventy-five miles long, one-half of which had been constructed, naturally with suitable safeguards. This enabled work on the StLAR to proceed, first with an American contractor but later by the company's own forces under the direction of another of the great civil engineers of early Canada, C. S. (later Sir Casimir) Gzowski. By July 1853 the line had been completed, the Canadian company having been capitalised at about £740,000. Almost one-half of this sum was raised

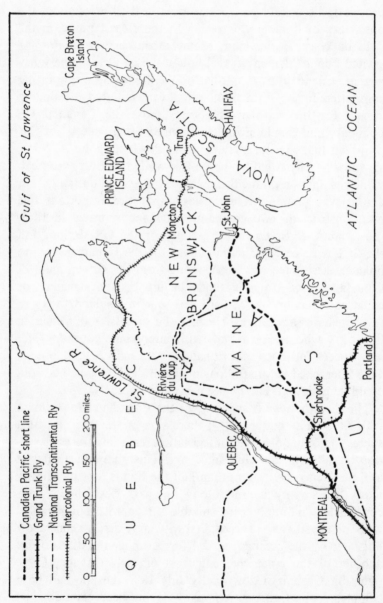

Map B: Montreal and rail routes to the sea

Legend:
- - - - - Canadian Pacific "short line"
──┼── Grand Trunk Rly
- - - - - National Transcontinental Rly
──┼── Intercolonial Rly

0   50   100   150   200 miles

through bonds backed by the government's guarantee. Even though the completed line stopped at Longueuil on the south shore of the St Lawrence, opposite the growing city of Montreal, it was still a most important route and was probably the first international railway. It was, in every way, the first Canadian 'trunk' line, a fact that was duly confirmed later when it became a part of the Grand Trunk system. It gave Montreal direct access to the sea during winter months when it could not function as a port. Even after rail connection was established with the Canadian Atlantic ports of Saint John and Halifax, the shorter distance to Portland (220 miles as compared with 480 to Saint John, for example) led to continued use of this international service, especially during winter months. The line is used today for freight traffic, its significance confirmed by the fact that an oil pipeline for the delivery of crude oil directly from ocean tankers to the refineries of Montreal parallels the route.

In 'Upper' Canada—the name was still used by Maritime citizens even though the two colonies of Canada were politically united—the pattern of constructing 'portage railways' continued on a rather grander scale than previously. Roughly parallel to the Ottawa & Prescott line was the Brockville & Pembroke Railway, joining Brockville on the St Lawrence with Pembroke to the Ottawa & Prescott line was the Brockville & Ottawa Railway, joining Brockville on the St Lawrence with Sand Point near Arnprior and on the shores of Chats Lake, by 1867. The railway company entered the steamship business on Chats Lake in competition with an established line of steamers, and bitter competition resulted. The inevitable amalgamation took place in 1868, a new steamship company taking over three competing interests. At the other end of this 75-mile line, a steep bluff obstructed direct access to the river front. A tunnel was therefore constructed, in 1860, so that the rails could be extended right down to a wharf. It is one-third of a mile long and still in good condition, still in occasional use. It remains the oldest tunnel in Canada and has the unique feature of having doors at each end.

Further to the west, a much more ambitious project had

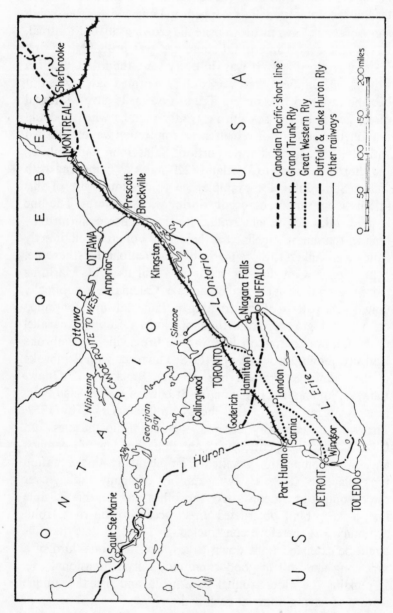

Map C: Railways in Canada West (now Ontario) ca 1860

been brought to completion a few years earlier, the first steam train in Upper Canada being hauled from Toronto twenty-five miles north to Aurora on 16 May 1853. This was the first section of what was known, for a time, as the Northern Railway which eventually ran from Toronto on Lake Ontario to Collingwood on Georgian Bay, Lake Huron, extension to this point being completed by 1855. In the words of the author of the classic volume on transportation in Canada the line was, as were other early Canadian railways 'suggested in the thirties, organised in the forties, and built in the fifties'. It followed a generally level route, one that had been used from the earliest days of travel in Canada as a portage from Lake Ontario to Lake Huron, thus eliminating the long journey round by way of Niagara Falls, up into Lake Erie, through Lake St Clair and so into the southern end of Lake Huron. The original portage had been from the site of Toronto, forty miles north to Lake Simcoe, and thence by small connecting rivers into Georgian Bay. The railway was naturally not limited to the shortest possible route and so was extended beyond the original portage to the shores of Georgian Bay, Collingwood being the final selection for the terminus. There were great hopes of capturing American trade, especially grain, coming down from the upper Great Lakes and to some extent this was realised. Other routes, however, took precedence but the Northern line performed notable service for three decades as part of the combined water-rail route to the Canadian West until the through rail route provided by the CPR was completed. The line remains in use today, as part of the CNR system, some indication of the changing scene being given by that fact that to many younger Canadians Collingwood is known mainly as the centre of a winter ski region.

The city of Buffalo, at the western end of the Erie canal system of the State of New York, was assuming importance at this time as a transhipment point. With the interest then shown by Canadians in developing transportation routes that would 'capture' some of the American trade, at least in winter months when water transport was not possible, another of the important railway projects of the fifties was the Great Western Railway (of Canada, that is), (GWR). This was a line to connect Niagara Falls and so Buffalo with the new towns growing up on the waterway connecting Lake Erie with Lake Huron, Detroit near the southern end and opposite the small Canadian town of Windsor, and Port Huron at the northern end opposite Sarnia. A spur line from Hamilton would connect Toronto with this interesting line that would provide through Canadian territory the shortest route between the two growing American cities. Connections were planned at the two ends with major US railways so that the Great Western Railway was also conceived as an international line, even though located wholly in Canada. The first sod was turned on 23 October 1849 but construction did not really get under way until 1851. The main line from the Suspension Bridge at Niagara Falls to Windsor was completed in January 1855, the connection to Toronto being finished in December of the year after. (Picture, p 36.) Its financing was greatly aided by the Guarantee Act of 1849.

There remained the great gap between Montreal and Toronto—a route of great potential importance which had not been overlooked by promoters. Two of the men active in the construction of the line to Portland were leaders in the chartering in 1851 of the Montreal & Kingston Railroad. Kingston was then relatively one of the most important cities of Canada, located at the foot of Lake Ontario, one terminus of the Rideau Canal by which it was connected with Bytown and still an important military centre. It is roughly half-way between Montreal and Toronto so that the idea of a rail link between the two cities was understandable. There were others with broader visions, however, one project being for a trunk line stretching 1,250 miles from Halifax to Hamilton. It was hoped—as usual, it might almost be said—to obtain a subsidy for this great project from the British Government but this was not to be. After delays while this possibility was being explored, work on the Montreal to Kingston line actually started in 1852.

Sir Francis Hincks, a senior minister in the Government of

Canada, had been in London in 1852 in connection with possible railroad financing. While there he came under the spell of William Jackson of the great contracting firm of Jackson, Brassey, Peto & Betts who were looking for fresh worlds to conquer. The company had already been actively seeking construction contracts in British North America, and Hincks agreed with Jackson that a company should be established for the purpose of building a railway from Montreal to Hamilton. The financing and actual start of construction of the Montreal and Kingston line complicated these plans but eventually Hincks introduced a bill to establish a Grand Trunk Railway Co (GTR), with authority to build a line from Montreal to Toronto. The Montreal and Kingston group were loud in their protests but waived their legal rights on the understanding that they would get a fair hearing. They were insistent that the complete project could be financed in Canada; the Grand Trunk group were equally insistent that this was impossible. The St Lawrence & Atlantic Co came into the picture but Hincks managed to solve this further impasse by promising that a bridge would be built across the St Lawrence at Montreal to connect their line with the Montreal to Toronto trunk route. The legislation setting up the Grand Trunk Railway Co was approved in 1852. The government were behind the British group and so control passed to London, England, a decision resulting in effects which are probably still felt in Canada today.

Jackson, Brassey, Peto & Betts built the line, which was opened from Montreal to Toronto in 1856. Construction was to high British standards but, lacking experience of Canadian winter conditions, the constructors encountered many difficulties. The route is a reasonably level one, paralleling the St Lawrence all the way for 330 miles, the only major bridges being two at the west end of the island of Montreal. These were well built, the piers being still in use today although the original iron tubular superstructures have long since been replaced. The StLAR was acquired on a 999-year lease.

Continuing on to the west of Toronto, an entirely new line was pushed through to Sarnia but avoiding Hamilton, despite the protests of the directors of the GWR who claimed, quite rightly, that their territory was being invaded. To the east, a line was built on the south shore of the St Lawrence, thus by-passing Quebec City (on the north shore), as far east as Riviére du Loup. And the St Lawrence was bridged at Montreal with the great Victoria tubular bridge, designed by Robert Stephenson. Even today this structure ranks among the great railroad bridges of North America. It is 9,144 ft between abutments, its original tubular superstructure being 6,592 ft long. The original piers are still in use but now carry a modern steel truss superstructure. (Picture, p 54.) With the opening of the bridge, a continuous rail connection was provided from the Atlantic seaboard at Portland to the US boundary at Sarnia. The modern era of Canadian railways had begun, the Montreal to Toronto line still being, in many respects, the 'main line' of Canada.

Not only did serious railroading in Canada start at the end of the fifties but so also did the long and tangled story of railway financing. This is a book about railways and not about money, but money was necessary—in large quantities—before railways could be built or operated. Most of the funds required for nineteenth-century railway construction in Canada came from British investors. Early railways around the world fell victim to the over-optimistic estimates of their promoters, and Canada, proving no exception, suffered a century of seemingly never-ending difficulties with regard to railway finance. By the early 1860s, all the pioneer railways of Canada were in trouble. Although the GWR had paid dividends starting in 1855, it, too, was in difficulty along with other lines, due largely to competition from the GTR. It was the financing of the Grand Trunk that was the major worry to the leaders of those times. Original promotional statements had included wonderful predictions of an interest rate of $11\frac{1}{2}$ per cent on capital, but by 1861 there was a deficit of £2,600,000, with more money still needed for completion. The overall situation was not improved by the report of the second of a long succession of Royal Commissions, this one appointed to look into the affairs of the GTR. The commissioners found inefficiency in management, fruitless competition with water routes, poor agreements with other companies, and deficiencies in construction, despite the high standards that were supposed to have been used and the relatively high unit cost of construction. Edward Watkin was sent over from England to take charge of affairs in Canada. It was clearly with his assistance that in 1862 the government passed a reorganisation bill that provided for a most ingenious rearrangement of the Grand Trunk's financial structure. The company was saved, and not for the first time.

From this capsule summary of some of the money troubles of 1860–61 something of the complexity of the situation can be gauged. It will be neither profitable nor of much interest to pursue the sordid financial story in greater detail so that only the major financial troubles of the years that followed will be touched upon. The elements of these future problems were all present, however, in 1860—poor estimates of construction costs, greatly exceeded when construction was complete; high operating ratios in view of the special difficulties of operation in Canada, winter conditions being but one of these; over-optimistic predictions of traffic potential; and a constant reliance upon governments to 'bail out' the companies which were otherwise bastions of the free-enterprise system. Indicative is the fact that the debt of the Province of Canada increased from about £3,800,000 in 1850 to over £10,800,000 at the end of the decade, much of this due to expenditure on canals, which were still in active use, and upon railroad construction.

Early hopes of being able to attract American business to the new Canadian lines were also beginning to fade and it was becoming increasingly clear that Canadian railways would have to stand on their own feet financially without indirect support from the more prosperous United States through payments for goods carried. This change from an international to a national outlook was inevitable in any case, as can now be seen so clearly, but it was strangely assisted by one of the most unusual chapters in Canadian railroad history, Canada's own 'battle of the gauges'.

CHAPTER 3

Battle of the Gauges: 1851-75

T he first railways in Canada were constructed, naturally and properly as can now be seen, to the Stephenson gauge of 4 ft 8½ in between rails. All the early railways in the northern part of the United States were similarly built to what soon came to be regarded as the 'standard gauge'. Rumours of the broad-gauge dispute in England may have reached Canada since, when the first railway Royal Commission was established in 1845 to investigate means of assisting railway construction, it was also charged with the task of selecting the gauge to be standardised throughout the Province of Canada.

At this time, the Portland to Montreal line was under construction, and being built to a rail gauge of 5 ft 6 in. One reason for this may possibly have been that the line started operations with two small locomotives (the *St Hyacinthe* and the *Beloeil*, names of Quebec towns served by the line) which are believed to have been purchased from the Arbroath & Forfar Railway in Scotland, built originally to this wide gauge. When, in 1851, the Royal Commission came to grapple with the gauge problem, the battle was on. The Portland interests marshalled the most remarkable arguments in favour of the adoption, as standard, of their own gauge of 5 ft 6 in, even going so far as to suggest that, since it would be different from that in general use in the United States, it would hamper any possible military invasion from the south! Memories of the war of 1812 were still vivid enough in some minds to render this a far from fanciful suggestion.

46

Other arguments are not worth repeating but they won the day, despite very strong objections from the GWR, based on the difficulties this change of its gauge would present to its anticipated American connections. On 31 July 1851 the Legislature of the Province of Canada passed an Act requiring the use of a rail gauge of 5 ft 6 in for all railways that were to receive assistance under the Guarantee Act of 1849; in effect, for all new railway construction in Canada. It would be thirty years before this lamentable legislation would be repealed; its effect upon Canadian railway development cannot now be estimated but it is clear from the records that it had a profound effect upon interchange traffic between Canadian and American railways at border points since all US lines in the vicinity of Canada were built with standard gauge. The GWR were forced to build their important line to what was now the 'provincial' gauge, thus creating difficulties for through traffic across the border at its two critically located end points, and this despite their strenuous objections.

The Champlain & St Lawrence Rail Road remained a standard-gauge line. Strangely, just six weeks after the fateful decision on the gauge question, a great celebration was held in Boston, Mass, to mark the first through train from Montreal to Boston by way of the little pioneer line, now extended to Rouses Point on the border, thence by new connecting US lines. The other early lines did not have to change but when the Grand Trunk line from Montreal to Toronto was built, it was provincial gauge throughout. The Bytown & Prescott line was built to standard gauge but the Guarantee Act did not apply to it since it was not seventy-five miles long and, in any case, it had decided upon standard gauge in order to make possible the development of a car-ferry service across the St Lawrence, between Prescott and Ogdensburgh, to connect up with the US line already described. But direct interchange of cars with the Grand Trunk Line would be impossible. Apart from one or two other even smaller lines, all new railway construction in the following critical years of railroad expansion in Canada was in conformity with the provincial gauge. By the year 1860, a total of 2,160 miles had been constructed, of which 92 per cent were 5 ft 6 in gauge lines.

The operating difficulties at transfer points with the United States can now only be imagined, and the wonder is that the first break in this quite ridiculous situation did not come earlier than it did. It was in 1864 that the GTR, as a part of its policy of absorbing existing lines whenever possible, gained control of the small system that had grown out of the original Champlain & St Lawrence line. This now included not only its original line, extended to Rouses Point, but the Montreal to Lachine line with a car-ferry service across the St Lawrence above the Lachine Rapids connecting with another line running down to Plattsburgh in New York State, also on Lake Champlain, all these lines being 4 ft 8½ in gauge. Significantly, no attempt was made by the Grand Trunk to change the gauge. A third rail was even laid across the Victoria Bridge for standard-gauge trains. To the west, in 1864, the GWR went to the expense of laying a third rail for the full length of their 229-mile line from Windsor to Suspension Bridge at Niagara Falls. This was the beginning of the end, even though it caused a great deal of trouble and extra expense, all mixed-gauge trains, for example, having to carry a large sign marked 'NG'.

It was not until 1870, however, that the parliament of what was now the Dominion of Canada took the inevitable step of passing the necessary legislation to repeal those parts of the 1851 Act that made use of the provincial gauge mandatory. The GWR (the coincidence of names is interesting) was ready for the change. On one day in December 1870 they narrowed the gauge of the branch from Hamilton to Toronto in the course of eight hours only; by mid-1871 they had removed the third rail from their main line, but due to delays in converting branch lines it was not until June 1873 that the GWR became a standard-gauge line throughout. The GTR started on the big job of conversion in November 1872 and within two years had completed the changeover, the conversion of the Inter-colonial Railway being completed by 1875. Inevitably there were a few dilatory smaller lines, but by the end of 1880 the task was substantially complete.

An interesting exception was the western extension of the Canada Central line (to be noted later) since it was built to broad gauge even in 1880 in order to use up discarded broad-gauge equipment. This was a temporary expedient, however, since by 1881 it had the necessary shops in which equipment could be converted so that it, too, became standard gauge. This left at the end of 1881 just sixty miles of broad-gauge line still in use. Forty-six of these miles were made up by the Cobourg, Peterborough & Marmora Railway, one of the several lines extending northward from the shores of Lake Ontario. Never really successful, it was abandoned completely in 1898. This left fourteen miles, those of the little portage railway at Carillon (page 26) still isolated from all other lines. And so it continued in its unique position as the only provincial-gauge line in Canada until it was finally closed about twenty years later.

Despite all these difficulties, the fledgling railways were operating and experience was being steadily gained, especially in countering winter conditions. Locomotives were generally imported from England and the United States but building in Canada started in 1853. As part of the Grand Trunk development there was built in the district of St Henri, Montreal, close to the island (northern) end of the new Victoria Bridge, the first major workshops of any Canadian railway. These, the Point St Charles shops, have been in continuous use ever since and their products have served Canada well. In May 1859 they turned out the grandest locomotive then to be seen on Canadian rails—No 209, a 4—4—0 weighing 48½ tons. After being run in, it had the honour of hauling the Royal Train of HRH the Prince of Wales in 1860 on his short ceremonial journey, most of his travel in Canada being by steamboat in keeping with the practice of that time.

The official inspector of Canada's railways, another well-known civil engineer, Samuel Keefer, included in his reports of the time statistics from which it is possible to give an overall picture of the locomotives and rolling stock in use in 1860. This summary table reflects, naturally, the dual-gauge situation and shows how dominant was the broad-gauge system. Locomotives totalled 395 divided as follows:

Built In:	Canada	Gt Britain	USA	Total
5 ft 6 in gauge	57	105	210	372
4 ft 8½ in gauge	—	4	19	23
Totals:	57	109	229	395

Rolling stock was of most varied kinds, inevitably so with the lack of any standardisation. The stock even included two sixteen-wheeled passenger cars, one built to serve as the Royal accommodation in 1860. There were thirty-seven twelve-wheeled passenger vehicles among the total of 490 cars, 90 per cent of the overall total being eight-wheelers. Only thirty-nine were for standard-gauge service, all the rest running on the provincial-gauge lines. Even more surprising is the variety of freight cars already acquired, including one 'refrigerator car' which must have been cooled by ice. Of the thirty-five snow ploughs already in use, only one was for the standard-gauge lines, and there were forty conductors' cars. About 85 per cent of all the freight rolling stock had eight wheels, an early indication of the major difference in practice between North American and British railways that still seems so remarkable to visitors. Only 6 per cent of the total of 5,874 freight vehicles listed for 31 December 1860 were for standard-gauge operations, another indication of the powerful position occupied by the 5 ft 6 in-gauge lines.

Probably the most significant contribution made by Canadian railways to rolling-stock development was the design and construction of the first sleeping car on any railroad. This was built in 1857 in the Hamilton shops of the GWR, the design being attributed to Samuel Sharp, the company's master mechanic. It is said that models of this unusual piece of equipment were sent to Great Britain and to France. Certain it is that the idea was adopted by the Pullman Company, whose first 'Pullman Car' appeared in 1859. Mails were first carried on Canadian trains in 1852, and, as elsewhere, the excellent service that rail transport provided was one of the main stimulants to the early improvement of postal service in general. Baggage cars were used in the first instance but eventually travelling post-office cars were built, some sixteen years after their development in England but ten years before they came into use in the United States.

Operating procedures were slow to develop to the high standards that have characterised railway working for so many recent decades. There were, therefore, some early accidents, including two very bad ones that were responsible for an acceleration in the development and promulgation of safety requirements. The worst was in 1864 at Beloeil, east of Montreal on the stLAR. It remains the worst accident in Canadian railroad history, 100 people losing their lives. The other was on the bridge over the small Desjardins Canal on the outskirts of Hamilton on the GWR line. It took place in the late afternoon of Thursday, 12 March 1857, when the 'fast express' from Toronto to Hamilton was nearing the end of its run. The bridge was not a large one, its span between masonry abutments being only 60 ft but its height above the icy surface of the canal was 40 ft. The train consisted of a locomotive, a baggage car and two passenger cars which were well filled. When the engine was retrieved some two weeks later and it was found that one of the driving wheels was broken, it was deduced that the broken wheel section or some other moving part had cut through the bridge timbers, precipitating all four vehicles on to the ice below. Since the couplings all broke, each car followed a different path before it sank through the ice. Sixty people lost their lives, only two dozen surviving, and so scattered was the population of Upper Canada at that time that it was said that there was not a town between Toronto and Windsor that did not have someone to mourn. Photographs were used, probably for the first time in such a case, to aid in the identification of victims, but the

Illustrated London News, reporting the accident a month later, printed the still standard type of engraving, prepared from a sketch made at the site of the disaster.

One of the passengers who died was a Samuel Zimmerman, a famous financier of the time. His record was a somewhat dubious one as a promoter and it was alleged that he was responsible for having secured the GWR's release from the requirement of having to stop all trains on either side of the Desjardins Bridge as a safety measure. Had this stop been made, the defective wheel would probably have been noticed and the accident averted.

Strict legislation was clearly necessary to govern railway operations and the first Act of this character, apart from those that granted original charters, was the Railway Clauses Consolidation Act passed by the Provincial Legislature in 1851. It did what its title suggested—consolidated the various and diverse clauses that had been appearing in individual railway Bills into a set of standard clauses that were to apply to all future railway construction. Companies, under this Act, were empowered to receive grants of land, build bridges, construct branch lines; surveys were to be controlled, valuation was to be standardised and specific requirements regarding fences and level crossings were to be met. Railways were, however, still permitted to fix their own rate structures. Regulation of charges was to come later, as were strict operating procedures, the two early accidents having the constructive effect of hastening this very necessary public control.

Page 53. (Above) *Eastbound transcontinental train of Canadian National Railways on southern section of its run from Cochrane to North Bay over the Temiskaming & Northern Ontario Railway in 1929; (below) typical lakeside station in British Columbia, showing one of the early* CPR *lake steamers and connecting train on Upper Arrow Lake, Arrowhead, in 1892*

Page 54. (Above) *Summer excursion train of the Algoma Central Railway seen at Agawa Canyon Station; (below) reconstruction of Victoria Bridge across the St Lawrence in the late 1890s. The original wrought iron tubular span is visible behind the new steel open truss span and the service loco-motive stands on a cantilevered extension now used for automobile traffic*

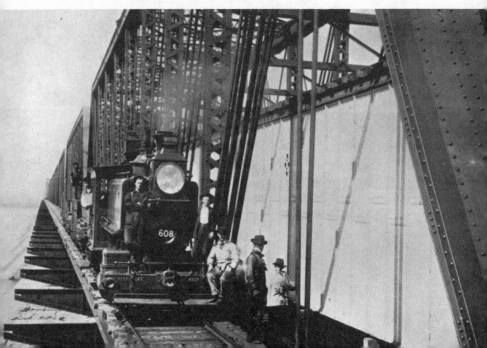

CHAPTER 4

The Intercolonial: 1858-76

In some ways, the 1860s constituted one of the most exciting decades in Canadian history. In its first year, Edward, Prince of Wales, paid the first Royal visit to British North America. Only a short time after the excitement of this visit had died down, the American Civil War broke out and for four years was of constant concern to Canadians. The murder of Abraham Lincoln in 1865 temporarily diverted attention from domestic affairs, but these had been in a state of turmoil for some time as earnest efforts were made to find some way of joining together the five separate mainland provinces. Confederation was finally achieved in 1867 and Canada became a country as well as a name. In November 1869, the 'Deed of Surrender' was signed by representatives of the Company of Adventurers of England trading into Hudson's Bay—the Hudson's Bay Company—releasing its long-time hold over the great central plains of Canada and of the Arctic, and giving to the young new country a challenge for its ultimate expansion that few if any other lands have ever experienced.

Of these exciting years one may read in innumerable excellent books. Throughout the decade, however, railway building provided a continuous theme that was featured in all the high-level policy discussions. Actual construction stood high in the economic activity of the provinces and then of the new dominion. Development of sound operation on the lines already built, and the consolidation of the GTR system, showed how valuable an asset well-managed railways could be in the steady development of the new land that the statesmanlike achievement of Confederation had at last made possible.

Early interest in rail communication in the Maritime Provinces has already been mentioned. The great disappointment of the mid-forties had not dampened enthusiasm for a rail connection between Halifax and Montreal and discussions continued intermittently, the urgency of the need for such a connection increasing as the years went by. The prospect of an eastern extension of the GTR to Riviére du Loup, and the successful completion of the railway between Halifax and Truro in 1858, would shorten the gap but there still remained 500 miles to be built if the northern route, recommended in 1848 by Major Robinson, was to be used. Discussions in the early sixties about the possibility of some form of union between the five provinces of British North America inevitably involved this railway dream, if only because almost all the travel of the delegates to the several conferences had to be by steamboat. In September 1864 the first formal conference was held in Charlottetown, Prince Edward Island, to be followed in October of the same year by the Quebec City Conference, at which the basic framework of Confederation was hammered out. The Westminster Palace Hotel in London was the scene of the final meeting. Then came the introduction of the necessary Bill in the British House of Commons and eventually the British North America Act became law, and the written constitution of the new dominion.

One of the most effective workers towards this end, though behind the scenes, was Edward Watkin of the GTR, later knighted by Queen Victoria. It is also to be noted that, as far back as 1839, Lord Durham had warmly recommended rail connection for the Maritime Provinces in his report to the British Government, one of the early great Canadian state papers.

Railways, and especially the Halifax to Montreal line which the GTR saw as a part of the Great Lakes to the sea line they were planning, loomed large in the discussions at Charlottetown and Quebec. It is, in fact, not too much to say that the Maritime Provinces would probably not have agreed to join with the

Province of Canada at that time had not the construction of this railroad been guaranteed. It was entirely appropriate that it should have been named, from the start, the Intercolonial. One of the resolutions adopted by the Quebec Conference was, therefore, that 'The General (ie, Dominion, when this name had been agreed upon) Government shall secure, without delay, the completion of the Intercolonial Railway from Rivière du Loup through New Brunswick to Truro, in Nova Scotia.' In the more sonorous language of the B.N.A. act, this agreement became Section 145, the opening words of which appeared at the start of this volume. So important is this clause of the Confederation Act that it warrants quotation in full, even in so summary a volume as this:

> Section 145. Inasmuch as the Provinces of Canada, Nova Scotia, and New Brunswick have joined in a Declaration that the construction of the Intercolonial Railway is essential to the Consolidation of the Union of British North America, and to the Assent thereto of Nova Scotia and New Brunswick, and have consequently agreed that Provision should be made for its immediate Construction by the Government of Canada: therefore, in order to give effect to that Agreement, it shall be the Duty of Government and Parliament of Canada to provide for the Commencement within Six Months after the Union, of a railway connecting the River St. Lawrence with the City of Halifax in Nova Scotia and for the Construction thereof, without Intermission, and the Completion thereof with all practicable speed.

Not a word about money! But it was known and well recognised that this was a political railway, in the very best sense, a line that would physically link together three widely separated parts of British North America; cost was secondary. Not a word about Prince Edward Island! But this tiny province, with an area of only 2,184 square miles, somewhat less than that of Devonshire, rejected the Quebec Conference resolutions, regarding expenditure upon the railway as an unwarranted addition to local taxation. It would not be until 1873 that 'The Island', as it is so happily known throughout Canada, agreed to join the union. And not until 1949, more than eighty years later, would Newfoundland become the tenth province of Canada.

Action, however, did not have to await all the legal procedures surrounding the final passage of the B.N.A. Act. As early as 1858 the Legislature of the Province of Canada had passed a resolution setting forth the national advantage to be gained by the building of a railway from Montreal to Halifax. Many meetings were held to discuss the proposal and deputations were sent over to England, with the usual objective of raising money, but the British Government, not surprisingly, refused to consider guaranteeing a loan until a survey of the route to be followed had been made. Misunderstandings arose even over this simple proposal but eventually the Provincial Government of Canada undertook the survey on its own, appointing in the spring of 1864 a civil engineer, Sandford Fleming, to undertake this task. His complete report was submitted in February 1865, a truly remarkable effort in view of the kind of country to be surveyed. But Fleming was a truly remarkable man.

Born in Kirkcaldy in 1827, Fleming came to Canada in 1845. He met Casimir Gzowski, one of the first great civil engineers of Canada, and so gained early railway experience, especially on the Ontario, Simcoe & Huron Railway, carrying out some notable early engineering work around Toronto. Placed in charge of the Intercolonial Railway surveys in 1863, he was appointed chief engineer of the Canadian Pacific Railway in 1871 and of the Newfoundland Railway in the same year, serving simultaneously in these three important posts. As will later be seen, he left the CPR in 1880 but was soon interested in other ventures, notably the laying of the first trans-Pacific cable, the success of which crowned his long and busy life. He designed the first Canadian postage stamp, founded the Royal Canadian Institute (one of Canada's oldest scientific bodies), and was responsible for the worldwide concept of time zones and Standard Time. As Sir Sandford Fleming and Chancellor of Queen's University he died, full of years and honours, at Halifax on 22 July 1915, truly one of the builders of Canada.

Not only did he direct all the surveys for the Intercolonial Railway prior to supervising its construction, but somehow he found time to write a full account of the whole vast project in a notable book. This is, therefore, one of the few early railway lines of Canada to be fully documented. There was much argument over the route to be followed, and Fleming carefully considered the many possibilities, as well as making detailed studies of the three main routes. A first glance at the map of eastern Canada suggests the 'obvious route' running due east from Montreal to Saint John in New Brunswick, thence round to Halifax. This was a route that could not be considered, however, since the Webster-Ashburton Treaty of 1847 had resulted in the international boundary taking its present erratic course, up almost to the St Lawrence, thus giving to the State of Maine a vast triangular area of forest land that should so logically have been a part of Canada. Fleming felt keenly about this, saying that 'No Canadian can reflect, without pain and humiliation, on the sacrifice of British interest in the settlement that was made. . . . The fault is due to the ignorance of the merits of the case and to an indifference to the interests at stake, on the part of the Imperial representative. . . .' For so 'political' a line as the Intercolonial, the route had naturally to be on Canadian soil throughout and so the northern route was selected, but the 'short line' from Montreal across Maine to Saint John was constructed twenty-five years later, being now a part of the CPR system and a serious competitor of the Intercolonial for through traffic almost from the time of its completion.

The northern route ran generally along the northern coast of New Brunswick with two big cut-offs across major peninsulas, then through the Matapedia Valley to the shores of the St Lawrence, along which a level route was easily selected to connect up with the existing Grand Trunk Line at Riviére du Loup. The Matapedia Valley section presented some problems of location, resulting in what is still one of the most beautiful stretches of railway in eastern Canada, but no major engineering works were involved apart from some large bridges across major rivers. Construction of the line, following Confederation, was financed by means of one of the first Acts of the Dominion

Parliament, authorising the raising of a loan of £4,000,000, the interest upon which was guaranteed, in a way, by the Imperial Government. The loan was oversubscribed four times but the actual cost of the line over-ran estimates by more than £2,800,000 so that additional financing had to be carried by the general accounts of Canada.

Four commissioners were appointed in 1868 to oversee construction but Fleming's position as chief engineer was directly confirmed by the government. One of the commissioners was C. J. Brydges, then managing director of the GTR, and many were the arguments between him and Fleming. Brydges wanted cheap construction but Fleming was determined to build well, foreseeing the long-term importance of this line. In some cases Fleming won the argument, as for example over the use of steel rather than timber for all bridges, even though the argument went as far as the Privy Council! The splendid masonry structures supporting the bridges and for other purposes that can still be seen and admired today are just as good as when built, through the excellent maintenance they have been given. CNR engineers of today have told the writer how greatly they admire the way that Fleming built, his high standards still minimising the need for maintenance almost a century later.

On the other hand, the commissioners had their way in insisting that all contracts for construction be relatively small in scope in order to spread the work, and on a lump sum rather than a unit-price basis, in which case volumes of material could have been adjusted as the true nature of each contract was revealed in actual construction. Fleming recounts the result of this decision. Of the twenty-three contracts awarded, only two were finished by the original contractor at his original price; two he does not mention; four were finished by the original contractor but at some increase in cost; but fifteen had to be taken out of the hands of the appointed contractor. Nine of these had to be completed by government forces; four were completed by other contractors, and two were passed on to other contractors but eventually they, too, had to be finished by government forces. The frustrations to Fleming in supervising contract work of this kind, over a route distance of 500 miles, can best be left to the imagination. Financial irregularities, for which he was in no way responsible, inevitably developed, so spoiling an otherwise splendid record.

The work was completed, however, by 1 July 1876 and Truro was connected by rail with Rivière du Loup and so with Quebec and Ontario (as Lower and Upper Canada were now known). Strangely, it was not decided whether the line should be operated by public authority or by a private company even when construction began. There are grounds for believing that, as late as 1870, Sir John A. Macdonald (the Prime Minister) was still thinking in terms of operation by the GTR. He must have changed his mind, however, for in 1874 the entire line was placed under the control of the Department of Public Works of the Canadian Government, which assumed the previous powers of the four commissioners. The Government purchased the sixty-one mile Nova Scotia Railway between Truro and Halifax, and later took over from the GTR that part of its line between Rivière du Loup and Levis, opposite Quebec City. In 1898 the final step was taken of purchasing the Drummond County Railway which gave access to the environs of Montreal, running powers over the Portland line of the Grand Trunk giving access to Bonaventure Station in the heart of Montreal. This same line remains today as a vital part of the CNR system, the Montreal to Halifax trains being the oldest of the longer cross-country services in Canada, with a total length of 840 miles.

Some important branch lines were constructed soon after the completion of the main line. One, in New Brunswick, went north from Bathurst to the small port of Shippegan. It was surveyed in 1873–74. When he wrote his book, Fleming still thought that it might 'provide a short mail route between England and America . . . only wharves and piers . . . are required to make the harbour available for the largest steamers.' Shippegan has, however, remained a small fishing port but the hopes once entertained for it were typical of the expectations of extensive rail traffic that were then widespread. The main line has always been well travelled but not to the extent of being a profitable railway. This low potential was realised from the outset, so the result was no real disappointment. The Intercolonial did what it was intended to do—forge a link between the Maritime Provinces and the rest of Canada, the reality of which can be felt even today as one rides the Ocean Limited from Halifax to Montreal.

When construction of the Intercolonial Railway started, Prince Edward Island was still outside the Confederation of Canada. In 1871 its legislature passed an Act for the construction of a railway from one end of the Island to the other with two branch lines later authorised, contractors to accept debentures in payment. The Act had specified the sum of £5,000 per mile as the payment to be made but did not specify the number of miles to be built. Contractors being but human, the result can be imagined. The original P.E.I. Railway must have held all records for the length of railway required to join any two places, all works such as embankments or cuttings being avoided by the simple expedient of using a curving alignment. Contractors also sold their debentures to local banks or pledged them against cash advances. So serious did the situation become that, despite continuing objections, the Island joined Confederation in 1873 on condition that the Government of Canada took over their railway and guaranteed regular operation of steam train ferry connections with the mainland across the seven-mile Northumberland Strait. This was the start of one of the busiest and most strategic train-ferry services that now form so important a part of the general rail system of the country. And the Island remains the only province of Canada that has been served only by a publicly-owned railway, the P.E.I. line now being a part of CNR.

Newfoundland, on the other hand, followed quite a different course. Granted responsible government in 1855, the people of the Island refused to join Confederation in 1867 or the succeeding years, and even in 1949 joined with Canada as its tenth province only by a slim majority. The story of the Newfoundland Railway is, therefore, really outside the purview of this book, which is just as well since its chequered history really requires a volume to itself. Since, however, it is now part of CNR, a bare outline of its development is desirable. In 1868, Sandford Fleming sent W. G. Bellaire to the Island to look over the country, so it was not surprising that the legislature, having voted a sum for a railway survey in 1875, asked Fleming to undertake this. He accepted, sent one of his chief assistants to direct the survey, the report on which was submitted within the year. A standard-gauge line was suggested, across the centre of the Island, to cost £1,600,000 but it was not built. Another survey was made in 1880 for a narrow-gauge line along the coast from St Johns, this time by men of a Canadian engineering firm. Indicative of Newfoundland politics of the time, and of many years thereafter, was the derogatory name 'The Canadian Cormorants' (come to pick our bones) given to the surveyors. The government decided to build the line, called for tenders, and awarded a contract to a syndicate of five men with the usual land grant but no guarantee of bonds; these were floated in London.

Work started in 1881; the first locomotives, built by the Hunslet Engine Co, were obtained secondhand from the P.E.I. Railway; the first train ran in June 1882 but in 1883 the syndicate defaulted. This was but the first act in a continuing drama of financial crises that really lasted until CNR had to assume control of 5,000 employees and a run-down 3 ft 6 in-gauge line on 1 April 1949. The UK bondholders, as mortgagees, did complete the initial line to Harbour Grace in 1884, the last spike being driven by a young midshipman from a British warship in St Johns Harbour, later King George V. The government did some further building on its own but had lawsuits with the bondholders which went as far as the Privy Council, finally buying them out in 1897. Prior to this a contract had been awarded in 1890 for an eastward extension of the line, the main contractor being R. G. (later Sir Robert) Reid who, with his sons, took over operation of the whole line in

1898 and precipitated one of the most vehement political fights in the Island's history, the contract being revoked by a new government in 1901. But the Reid company remained and did operate the railway until 1923 when the government finally took it over, the Reids being said to have lost £1,200,000 through the years in keeping the line going.

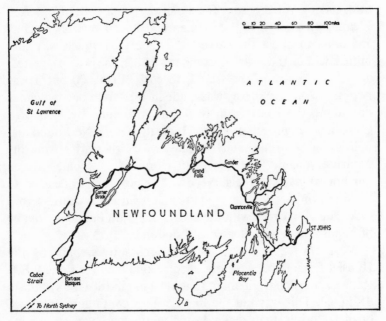

Map D: The Newfoundland Railway (now CNR)

The railway eventually did cross the Island, however, the first train to Port aux Basques leaving St Johns on 29 June 1898, and the first connecting boat arriving at North Sydney on 1 July. Total length of line operated was 906 miles, of which the main line accounted for 548 miles. An error in location took the line over Gaff Topsail, a high, barren, wind-blown waste, operation across which produced legendary problems (all trains having to carry chains to hold them to the rails if gales were encountered). Since no roads existed, the railway was the lifeline of the Island but carried little freight, only 300,000 tons in 1930. In 1945, however, it carried seven million tons, mainly war supplies, but maintenance was neglected so that in 1949 Canada took over a real liability, renovation being a costly procedure.

CHAPTER 5

Surveys for the Transcontinental Railway: 1872-80

The story of transportation to the west coast of Canada starts with the great canoe journey of Alexander Mackenzie who, on 22 July 1793, first reached the Pacific coast overland from Canada, missing a possible rendezvous with Capt Vancouver, RN, then exploring the coast, by less than two weeks. Other great travellers of the fur trade followed Mackenzie's lead, so that by the early years of the nineteenth century links were already being forged between the few settlers on the west coast and the well-established colonies in the east. And as early as 1829, Sir Richard Bonnycastle, an officer of the Royal Engineers who came to know the Canadas well, suggested the idea of a railway connection from coast to coast. Men of the two companies of this same notable corps who were sent to what is now British Columbia in the fall of 1858, and who did so much in laying the foundations of civil life on the Pacific coast, must similarly have dreamed of a railway through the mountains and on to the east as they laboured at their fantastic road construction up the Fraser River canyon.

Travel from coast to coast, by canoe, was stimulated by the remarkable journeys of Sir George Simpson, Governor of the Hudson's Bay Company under whose jurisdiction the west still remained. Once railways had come to be accepted in the east, it was but natural that quite serious proposals should have been advanced for a transcontinental railway line. The first specific suggestion advanced to the Government of the Province of Canada was made in 1851, being promptly sent to a committee of the Legislature for study. This was the beginning of political considerations of trans-Canada railways that would continue unabated for well over half a century. In inception and prosecution, the Intercolonial Railway was a political line; the Canadian Pacific initially was even more so.

The key to the west in those days was the Hudson's Bay Company, still operating under its original charter. In 1857 the British Government established a select committee of the House of Commons 'to consider the State of those British Possessions in North America which are under the Administration of the Hudson's Bay Company. . . .' and this proved to be the 'beginning of the end' for the great company as a territorial power. Amongst those who gave evidence to this committee was John Ross, then president of the GTR, whose testimony naturally anticipated an extension of his line to the west. This company's interest in the Intercolonial was similarly related to its expansionist ideas; it was certainly in the background of many of the discussions in the immediately succeeding years. In 1858 gold was discovered on the Fraser River and the consequent gold rush served to accelerate not only the development of civil government for the western settlement but also the idea of the necessity for a railway connection with the east. Possibly by coincidence, it was in the same year that Sandford Fleming voiced his hopes for such a railway in a public lecture saying *inter alia* that: 'The construction of the Pacific Railway is a work of the grandest magnitude and perhaps of universal importance . . . (it) would tie with a band of iron the interests and affection of (Britain's) subjects in Europe, Asia and America, to colonise half a continent, and to complete the foundation of her Canadian Empire.'

In 1866 the two small colonies of Vancouver Island and (mainland) British Columbia were united under the name of the latter. Almost immediately, the idea was raised of the united colony joining with those in the east in the Confederation that was to be Canada, but there was still the problem of the Hudson's Bay Company. In 1863, however, GTR interests had finally gained control of this venerable chartered company; a new governor and board now directed its interests. And the new policy soon led to a release of its ancient land-holding rights, the actual 'Deed of Surrender' being signed by officials of the company in 1869. The way was now clear for an opening-up of the west. Settlers in the Red River colony (around what is now the city of Winnipeg) had not waited for this clearance, however, but had petitioned the Provincial Government as early as 1863 for the construction of a railway that would link them to the east and also to the west coast. There were assuredly men of vision, or dreamers if you will, in those turbulent days of Canada's political history.

When, therefore, a delegation from British Columbia sat down with ministers of the new country of Canada to discuss entering Confederation, the construction of a railroad to the west coast had high priority. So anxious were the westerners to have this transportation link that they suggested as a temporary expedient that a railway might be built as far as the foothills of the Rocky Mountains and a colonisation roadway thence to the coast. Sir George Etienne Cartier, a true statesman, turned down this idea completely, suggesting that the day would come when Canada would need three transcontinental railways to carry all the traffic of the country—an unfortunate prophecy as it turned out to be, but an action indicating clearly his faith in the future of the newly constituted country.

In the final agreement under which British Columbia did enter Confederation there appeared this significant undertaking: 'The Government of the Dominion undertakes to secure commencement simultaneously within two years from the date of Union, of the construction of a railway from the Pacific towards the Rocky Mountains, and from such point as may be selected east of the Rocky Mountains towards the Pacific, to connect the seaboard of British Columbia with the railway system of Canada; and further, to secure the completion of such railway within ten years from the date of Union.'

The die was cast. The leaders of the new nation had committed themselves and their limited resources to the building of a railway across almost a thousand miles of relatively unknown virgin forest land north of the Great Lakes, over another thousand miles of prairie, and finally through the 600-mile barrier formed by the triple mountain chains, the Rockies, the Selkirks and the Coast Ranges. Naturally, there was much criticism of what some regarded as utter folly, just as there was praise from others for the courageous decision that had been made. And just as today, when new rail links have to be provided, there are always those coming forward with dubious alternatives (such as monorails) to well-tried rail transport, so also were there alternatives proposed to a railway even to the west coast. One gentleman proposed a 'perpetual sleigh road' capable of carrying passengers at speeds up to 100 mph, giving a crossing of the continent in from forty to forty-five hours. The Government of Canada, however, was not diverted by such suggestions and decided upon an immediate reconnaisance of the route that would have to be used, to be followed by detailed surveys. They decided to place this onerous task in the hands of one who had already proved his merit, Sandford Fleming.

Although still actively in charge of the building of the Intercolonial, Fleming had this work so well organised that he was able to undertake this new assignment as well. On 16 July 1872, he set off from Toronto with a small party to cross the continent. Included in his party, most fortunately, was a Dr George M. Grant (later Principal of Queen's University, Kingston) who kept careful notes which he skilfully wove into one of the most famous of early Canadian travel books, *Ocean to Ocean*. They went by train to Collingwood (p 41) thence by boat to the head of Lake Superior. They then travelled over the 'Dawson Road' and through the forests and lakes that had to be traversed before the open lands of the prairies were reached, getting to Fort Garry (Winnipeg) on 31 July. Then by cart and pack horse to Jasper House, west of Edmonton, reached on 2 September. Before the end of the month, with their good guides and fine equipment, they had penetrated the mountains, through the Yellowhead Pass, and had reached the first settlers' houses at Kamloops on the Thompson River. The trail through the Yellowhead Pass was now well marked but the journey was still a real pioneering effort, not to be undertaken by any but a well equipped and guided party. That part of the route between what is now North Bay and the head of Lake Superior was still untravelled country, all journeys to the west avoiding this rough country by boat travel on the lakes in summer, and over the ice in winter. Fleming knew this well, however, so that he was well prepared to organise the great task of surveying the route. This was commenced in 1873, and continued through the next six years, a survey that did far more for the development of western Canada than merely providing the basis for selecting the route of the railway to the west.

Even today, and even to those who are familiar with the terrain that had then to be traversed in its modern condition, the work of Sandford Fleming and his loyal staff in conducting this great survey in relatively so short a time and so economically remains an almost unbelievable achievement. The total population of British North America at the time was no more than three and a half million, only 23,000 of whom lived west of Lake Superior, and even they were generally congregated in the few settlements that then existed. Through this empty land routes had to be discovered and lines had to be run, and to do this supplies had to be transported and information transmitted so that work in different parts could be co-ordinated all over great distances. Winter conditions with temperatures for weeks well below −20°C had to be faced and, equally bad if not worse, the torrid heat of high summer with its humidity and incredible menace of biting flies. Nothing can convey to readers who have not been in the 'Canadian bush' in high summer what flies can be like—generally mosquitoes and black flies—so the human discomforts of this great transcontinental survey must be left to the imagination. Despite all difficulties, however, 46,000 miles of lines were studied on foot in reconnaisance surveys, and 11,500 miles were surveyed in detail with instruments and duly recorded.

Page 71. *Southbound freight train of the Pacific Great Eastern Railway (now British Columbia Railway) on the rocky shore of Howe Sound between Squamish and North Vancouver*

Page 72. (Above) *The Museum Train, assembled by Canadian National Railways, that toured Canada coast-to-coast in 1955–6;* (below) *locomotives outside the first train shed of the Canadian Railway Museum at St Constant, Quebec, of the Canadian Railroad Historical Association*

To achieve this result, Fleming used the experience he had gained in his initial work on the Intercolonial. The whole survey was divided into three main regions—the Woodland (from Upper Canada to the prairies), the Prairie and the Mountain Regions. Interestingly enough, the latter two names are used in the same way and for roughly the same areas by CNR for its operations today. Twenty-one divisions were then organised under the three regions, with suitable delegation of responsibility to the fine staff that Fleming was able to recruit so quickly. He made his own headquarters in Ottawa which really represented the eastern end of the trans-continental line that had to be surveyed, railways only then being built up the Ottawa River valley. He had 800 men at work in the first survey season, the number increasing to about 2,000 in later seasons. The supply problems alone for such survey crews, spread out over almost 3,000 miles of country, were monumental. Although work in the mountains might appear to have been the most spectacular, probably the most difficult section of the entire route was in the forested lake-and-stream country north of Lake Superior. Forest fires were a continual menace; in one bad fire seven men lost their lives. Fast-flowing rivers, with unknown rapids, had to be crossed as well as used for transport; in the second survey season twelve men lost their lives through drowning. And muskegs innumerable had to be crossed in survey work and avoided if possible in route location—'muskeg' being an Indian word used in Canada to describe bogs of recently formed organic material, always dangerous in view of the high water content and depth of even the most stable muskegs.

The surveys were completed, however, and routes selected— in the final phase by Fleming himself. Discarding a first choice for the location north of Lake Superior that went inland, north of Lake Nipigon, he recommended a route along the shore of Lake Superior and this was almost exactly the route finally used by the CPR. His choice across the prairies took the line past Edmonton in heading for the Yellowhead Pass. The CPR later used a more southernly route for their passage through the mountains. Fleming's location, however, was later to be used by the two other transcontinental railways so that, in effect, he was responsible for the location of the CNR lines that cross Canada from Halifax to Vancouver. Beyond the Yellowhead Pass there was a wide choice of routes, all difficult. Fleming finally decided, quite apart from all the local pressures that must have been exerted upon him, that the route down the Thompson and Fraser River valleys to Burrard Inlet was the one to be followed, Burrard Inlet being the site of the Vancouver of today, subsequently selected by the CPR for their Pacific terminus. Fleming's route is that followed today by the CNR into Vancouver; one of the other routes that his crews investigated is that used by the CNR line to Prince Rupert. This decision, about the final western part of the route, was made in the summer of 1878; it could be said to mark the completion of one of the greatest surveying projects ever undertaken in North America, if not in the world.

The building of the railway had naturally been under active discussion since the very start of survey work. For ten years it was to provide the prime topic of political discussion in Canada, being largely responsible for the fall of the Conservative government in 1873, followed by a brief but significant reign of power at Ottawa for the Liberal party. Early in the chequered story, the GTR eliminated themselves, despite their earlier activity, by refusing to have anything to do with the construction of a railway around Lake Superior saying that '. . . (it) could not be built except at tremendous cost, when built it could not be worked successfully in winter, and if it could be worked would have no traffic to carry upon it.' They were probably right, at the time, but there were men in positions of power, notably Sir John A. Macdonald, Canada's first Prime Minister, who could see beyond the difficulties of the time and who realised that this most difficult section of line— long, expensive and unremunerative though it might be— would be essential if the Pacific railway were truly to tie together the separated parts of the new country. Two groups started negotiating for the charter to build the railway, and for months they ran on parallel courses. Eventually the government, maintaining a strictly neutral attitude, passed Acts granting charters to each in 1872, the Interoceanic Railway Co and the Canada Pacific Railway Co, the Acts being almost identical. Attempts were made to amalgamate the two projects but these failed, one of the major complications being the dominance of US interests in one of the companies.

In February 1873 a new attempt was made by the government in the preparation of a charter, the preamble to which refers to the failure to amalgamate the earlier efforts. Some of the men involved in these abortive attempts were named as subscribers in the new charter (as were Walter Shanley and Sandford Fleming) which called for a capitalisation of ten million dollars, a start within two years, and completion within ten. Raising the capital was rather more difficult than preparing the charter; the normal difficulties were compounded by what is still known in Canadian history as the 'Pacific Scandal'. In the general election of 1872, the Conservatives were returned to power but with a reduced majority, in view of Liberal gains. Soon after the new session started, a Liberal MP introduced a resolution in which it was stated that certain monies had been paid by Sir Hugh Allan of Montreal, leader of the organisers of the new company, in connection with the organisation of the company and in a way that reflected upon the government. It became clear that money had been given to the Conservative party, Macdonald's demands for help having been put on paper. A Royal Commission of three judges was appointed in August 1873 and the political storm increased with the publication in Montreal newspapers of incriminating letters, said to have been copied from originals purloined from private offices. The Royal Commission sat in September and October but on 5 November, in the face of the allegations of corruption, the government resigned with the charges unproven.

The new Liberal government that took office was headed by Alexander Mackenzie who served as Minister of Public Works as well as Prime Minister, thus being directly responsible for railway matters. A cautious Scots Canadian, he faced a most difficult situation; agitation in British Columbia for the promised railway connection was steadily mounting, yet construction had not even started. Raising capital for the Pacific railway proved to be impossible for a variety of reasons. Neither the Liberal nor the Conservative parties wanted to depart from the principle of having the railway built by private enterprise, but while the Liberals were anxious to proceed slowly, taking the ten-year completion period as a goal to aim at rather than as a commitment, the Conservatives were anxious to see the whole line built as quickly as possible. Eventually, however, the Liberal government was forced to the conclusion that construction must be started and that this would have to be done under direct governmental supervision. And Sandford Fleming was naturally given this additional burden.

The basic idea seems to have been to build those sections of the line for which surveys had been completed and which would give access to strategic points in association with water transport. No attempt, therefore, was made at any construction eastward from Fort William, at the head of Lake Superior. The Red River provided access to the Canadian prairies from the south and there was the beginnings of a real settlement at Fort Garry (Winnipeg) from which lines could be constructed running both east and west. The small settlement on the Pacific coast would naturally have to be connected by rail through the mountains so that a start on the coast, to which supplies could be delivered by sea, was a fourth possibility.

Contracts for construction of the line running west from Fort William were let, starting in 1875. Even though supplies could be so easily delivered to the Lakehead by boat through the Great Lakes, the country to be traversed to reach the Red River was still the forbidding Precambrian terrain for about 300 miles, a land of innumerable streams, lakes and muskegs, and this had to be crossed before the more open prairie country was reached. By 1880, however, the whole length between Fort William and Selkirk on the Red River was complete. Selkirk was Fleming's choice for the crossing of the Red River; it is about sixteen miles downstream from the location chosen later for the crossing of the CPR at a point where the Assiniboine River joins the Red and which is today the centre of the great city of Winnipeg. In some ways it is regrettable that Selkirk did not become the major centre. Across the river from Winnipeg is the city of St Boniface and it was from this small settlement that the first 'official' train for the east left on 10 February 1880 to run as far as Fort William where there was now a sizeable railway depot, even including a locomotive roundhouse. Following the example of Montreal, an ice railway had been operated across the frozen surface of the Red River during one or two winters prior to 1880, but in the summer of that year a timber pile bridge was completed and the first freight train to cross the river did so on 26 August.

Construction west of the Red River was, prior to this date, dependent upon supplies coming up from the United States and so it was this southern route that was the pioneer railway of western Canada. Railways had been pushed across the broad plains of the States starting in the sixties, so that it was possible in the seventies to travel from the Atlantic coast by rail, albeit slowly, to Fargo, North Dakota, located on the Red River. Boat travel down the river could then be used to gain access to the Red River settlement of Canada in summertime, and a stage service when navigation ceased for the year. This route was used by officers of the Hudson's Bay Company on their journeys to the west as early as 1865 instead of the long canoe journey up the Ottawa River and through the Great Lakes to Fort William, followed by the 400-mile canoe route through the Lake of the Woods area. A railway connection to the south, parallel to the Red River, was therefore an obvious first link in western rail transport. Government construction of this line, long known as the Pembina branch, started with the award of the first contract in 1874. It was not completed until December 1878, the first train running on the second day of that month from St Boniface southward to St Vincent, Minnesota, a small point on the US side of the border where connection was made with the Saint Paul & Pacific Railroad.

The unusual direction of this train is explained by the fact that a locomotive had been delivered to St Boniface in 1877 to work on the construction of the branch. This was the *Countess of Dufferin*, now labelled as CPR locomotive No 1, and on permanent exhibition in Winnipeg. Built by Baldwin's in Philadelphia in 1872, she was later purchased for the work in Canada. Loaded on to a barge at Fargo, she was brought down the Red River by the sternwheeler *Selkirk*, receiving a gun salute from the US garrison at Fort Pembina as she passed. On the 10 October the strange little flotilla passed Winnipeg with the whistles of both the *Selkirk* and the locomotive sounding shrilly, since steam pressure had been built up in its boiler to salute the auspicious occasion. Rails had been run to the water's edge at Point Douglas, near St Boniface, on the east bank of the river, and here the first locomotive of western Canada was safely landed. By a truly remarkable coincidence, the locomotive had been bought by Joseph Whitehead, one of the railway contractors, who is said to have served as the fireman on the engine that hauled the first train for public passenger service on the Stockton & Darlington Railway in 1825, in such contrast to this later experience on the open prairie land of Canada. The *Countess of Dufferin* (named after the wife of the Governor-General of Canada at the time), after serving well on the Pembina branch was sold to a lumber firm in Golden, B.C., in 1897, working there at shunting duties until purchased and presented to the City of Winnipeg in 1911. She was joined in the winter of 1879 by a second locomotive that had come up from Fort William, but regular service on the branch line started very shortly after the historic first journey. The immediate value of this link with the 'outside world' can well be imagined. Opening-up of the west really started from this time, a development that still continues.

With this connection to the south, and the imminence of rail connection across the Red River, it was possible to start construction of the Pacific railway to the west of Selkirk. By 1880, about one hundred miles had been constructed. A start in British Columbia was a more formidable undertaking, but early in 1880 a contract was awarded to Andrew Onderdonk for the commencement of this great task. A party of twenty-one engineers left Ottawa on 19 March 1880 and travelled to the west coast by GTR to Chicago, thence by the single transcontinental railway then completed (the Union Pacific and Central Pacific lines) to San Francisco. Boat travel was then necessary up to British Columbia, the whole journey taking nine days. The initial blast to mark the start of this major construction project was fired at Yale (on the Fraser River near the start of the mountains) on 14 May 1880. By the end of the year over one hundred miles of rail had been laid in British Columbia, but this was only a small beginning of one of the greatest pieces of railway construction ever to be undertaken. Between 1871 and 1879, over $14 million had been spent by the government on this very difficult portion of the Pacific railway. It is not surprising to find that even so great a man as Fleming could not stand the strain of directing this continent-wide operation, especially with the government interference to which he was subjected (as was later revealed). He had been forced to take leave of absence for health reasons and on his return to work found his staff demoralised and much of the work in rather less than a satisfactory state.

Throughout all these years, the political pot had been kept boiling in a manner that makes modern political developments seem unusually tame. The Conservatives mounted a singularly active opposition to the Liberal administration of Alexander Mackenzie, but a general election was not called until late in 1878. The Conservatives, still under Sir John A. Macdonald, were returned to power and took office on 17 October of that year. Indicative of the importance that railway construction occupied in the highest quarters and also of the political rancour of the time was the fact that one of Sir John Macdonald's first actions was to cancel Fleming's carefully considered decision to use the Yellowhead Pass for the route through the mountains of the Pacific railway, only to have to reinstate the decision in 1879. Politics being what they were in those days, however, a Royal Commission was appointed in June 1880 to examine the whole railway situation. Charges had naturally been made about the slow progress achieved under the Liberal government and there were the inevitable suggestions of mismanagement. The commission presented a three-volume report in 1882 that makes interesting if somewhat distressing reading today, since it is clear that the commissioners could have had little idea of the difficulties with which the field crews had to contend.

Even before this, however, Fleming—despite his original appointment by a Conservative government but consequent upon his loyal service under the Liberal administration—was criticised. In March 1880 charges against him were made in the House of Commons, charges that he could not answer directly and that were clearly unfounded. He was removed from his office as engineer-in-chief by an Order in Council of 22 May and, quite naturally under the circumstances, refused to accept the substitute position of consulting engineer and so his services were lost to the great project the foundations of which he had so well and truly laid. He had the satisfaction of knowing that the major surveys had been completed and that he was leaving behind over 700 miles of railway in operating condition.

Fleming was clearly the victim of political circumstances, notably the appointment of contractors for political reasons. He went on, however, to other and even more far-reaching services, and today the whole world is in his debt for his invention and promotion of the concept of Standard Time. His railway work readily explains his interest in achieving some regularity in the changes in time that have to be made as one travels east or west over such great distances as North America presents. Today, the convenience of Standard Time zones is so commonplace that it is difficult to realise the chaotic situation that existed until regularised initially by the almost single-handed efforts of this great Scots Canadian.

CHAPTER 6

Building the C.P.R: 1881-86

The Conservative Government of 1878 was forced by commitment to continue construction of the Pacific railway under its own supervision for the first two years of its period in office, despite its earlier efforts to have the work done through private enterprise. Sir Charles Tupper, the Minister of Public Works and so responsible for railways, as he was also after a separate Ministry of Railways and Canals had been formed in 1879, actually awarded the last contract, that to Andrew Onderdonck for the start of construction from the west coast. But behind the scenes negotiations were soon under way for an alternative to this procedure. A mission was, of course, sent to England to see if the British Government would join financially in a land-holding commission, proceeds from the sales of which would pay for the railway. London was not responsive. Discussions were then started with two independent groups, one headed by the Earl of Dunsmore involving English capital, the other more or less Canadian group being headed by D. J. McIntyre and George Stephen a Canadian who, with his associates, had made a fortune out of the St Paul, Minneapolis & Manitoba Railway. Nothing was actually done, however, until a delegation of three, headed by the Prime Minister, Sir John A. Macdonald himself, went over to London in July 1880, to receive tenders from interested groups. They interviewed Sir Henry Tyler, then president of the GTR, but he would have nothing to do with the proposal if it was to include a line around Lake Superior. Macdonald, with that vision that so distinguished his

81

public career, was determined that it would and so the GTR faded from the picture for over a quarter of a century. There were no direct results from this overseas journey but in August of the same year McIntyre submitted a new proposal to the government.

The group offered to build the railway for a cash grant of $25 million and a grant of free land of twenty-five million acres. The government accepted the proposal and a contract was signed on 21 October. It was introduced into the House of Commons for approval on 10 December, and there followed one of the longest and most acrimonious debates that had yet featured in the proceedings of the new Parliament. When the formal agreement was eventually approved by Parliament it included other provisions of great benefit to the proposed company. The subsidies were to be paid in instalments based on each twenty miles of line completed; the land was to be granted in alternate sections and any land not fit for settlement would be replaced by land elsewhere; land for railways shops, buildings, etc, was to be free; the government would complete and turn over to the CPR the lines already built; all materials for original construction could be imported free of duty; the railway with its grounds and buildings and the company's capital were to be free of taxation; the land grants were also to be free of taxation for twenty years unless sold; and for twenty years no railway would be permitted south of the new line with one limited exception. The company was also to be allowed to issue $25 million in bonds using the land granted as security.

The concept of land grants on such a lavish scale will appear somewhat strange to non-Canadian readers, but this was in the days when the 'open prairie' seemed to be almost limitless and was so empty of people that any use for it must have appeared then to be sound. The same system had been followed in the early days of railway construction in the western USA but the last land grants had been made there in 1871. Montreal interests dominated the proposed board of directors. This led to a revival of the old Montreal-Toronto rivalry, and even to the submission of a counter proposal from a Toronto-based group, but the original proposal was ratified by Parliament on 16 February 1881 and the formation of the Canadian Pacific Railway Co received Royal assent the next day.

So began one of the great railway-building epics of all time. Given ten years to complete the line, the new company were to finish it within four and a half years, regular service between Montreal and the Pacific coast starting in but little more than five years from the day on which the first sod had been turned— 2 May 1881. All this was done in the face of almost continuous financial difficulties and with sustained and vociferous opposition from many important quarters not only in Canada but in Great Britain. It is interesting today to read what *Truth*, an influential British journal of the time, had to say:

> 'Canadian Pacific, if it is ever finished, will run through a country about as forbidding as any on earth . . . British Columbia is not worth keeping. It should never have been inhabited at all . . . in Manitoba those who are not frozen to death are often maimed for life by frostbites. Ontario is poor and crushed with debt. It is certain to go over to the States and when that day comes the Dominion will disappear.'

An interesting prophecy, fortunately wrong in all respects.

The opposition of the Liberal party was based on rather more factual evidence but the criticism was, in the long run, singularly unfortunate since it created the idea that the Liberal party, as such, was opposed to the CPR and all that it stood for. This idea carried with it the implicit suggestion that something would be necessary to balance this first transcontinental railway. When the Liberals started their long reign in Ottawa, in 1896, this vague idea proceeded to bear strange fruit.

Sir George Stephen gave up the presidency of the Bank of Montreal in order to lead the new company. Associated with him as directors were Duncan McIntyre, Richard B. Angus, Donald A. Smith, John S. Kennedy and James J. Hill, the latter an almost mythical figure in US railway history even though he was a Canadian. He was anxious to see the CPR follow the route favoured by the GTR by going to Sault Ste Marie, making connection there with one of his US lines running south of Lake Superior, thus avoiding the formidable task of building the 'Woodland' section in Canada. When it became clear that the new line was indeed to be an all-Canadian line, despite the difficulties of the Lake Superior section, 'Jim' Hill left the board. Before his departure, however, he had made one contribution for which Canada will always be grateful. He had recommended and finalised the appointment of William Cornelius Van Horne as general manager of the Canadian Pacific. There has probably never been a better example of 'the right man, in the right place, at the right time'.

It was Van Horne's genius and capacity for seemingly superhuman work that led to the surmounting of all difficulties and the completion of the CPR to the west coast in so phenomenally short a time. He was American-born, starting his railway work as a telegraph operator on the Illinois Central at the age of fourteen. He rose rapidly, one of his early successful ventures being to restore the bankrupt Southern Minnesota Railroad to economic health. He was serving with the Chicago, Milwaukee & St Paul line when spotted by Hill, whose own operations bordered on this already important line. He took up his office at Winnipeg on 1 January 1882. He was to serve the rest of his life in Canada, as a Canadian, being knighted by Queen Victoria for his services and finishing his days as one of Montreal's most honoured citizens. But before that, he was to show what the organising ability and inspired leadership of one great man could do in the wilds of Canada.

One of Van Horne's early accomplishments was to have the company appoint Thomas G. Shaughnessy as assistant general manager. He was stationed in Montreal in charge of all purchasing and soon proved to be an outstanding supply officer. With Van Horne in command of what can well be called 'field operations', Shaughnessy making sure that his incredible demands for supplies were always met, and Sir George Stephen finding—often with great difficulty—the necessary funds to keep operations going at the pace set by Van Horne, the stage was set for the construction drama that is today known around the world. Within the confines of this short volume all that can be done is to explain what was accomplished, with brief reference to some of the highlights, leaving readers who wish to know more about the wonderful human story of the 'Building of the CPR' to refer to one or other of the fine books whose titles are listed on page 237.

The start in 1882 was delayed by one of the occasional great spring floods on the Red River, one of the worst on record until the disaster of 1950. But Van Horne soon had 5,000 men at work on the prairies with 1,700 teams of horses, mechanical construction equipment still being a promise of the future. Surveys were pushed forward north of Lake Superior to locate with finality the difficult, and still controversial, 'Woodland' section. Surveys were conducted in the mountains, the most difficult part of this work being the finding of a passage through the Rocky and Selkirk Mountains since it had been decided to locate the mountain section of the line well to the south of the Yellowhead Pass—in order, it is said, to obviate for all time the possibility of any US line drawing traffic away from that part of Canada close to the border. A pass through the Selkirks was found by Major Rogers and it carries his name today.

Meantime, the government had passed over to the company, as a gift, the lines already completed under government construction control. These were officially valued at $27,700,000, making the total grant well over fifty million dollars, plus the twenty-five million acres of land. Even with this magnificent running start, the company was soon in financial difficulties. Again and again the end of the supply of money seemed to be in sight; again and again Stephen with his wide contacts and aided immeasurably by the reluctant but effective support of Sir John A. Macdonald was able to raise the needed additional capital. The tale of this 'frenzied finance' (to use a title of Stephen Leacock's that is indeed applicable) could fill many books. Suffice to say that the work was never stopped and the great task was completed, even though at the end the directors had pledged their own private fortunes to ensure the essential capital. They were well repaid. Dividends started slowly late in 1885, 3 per cent being paid from 1885 to 1888, then rising to 4 and eventually 5 per cent in 1890, but not to 6 per cent until 1905. By that time, the initial financial problems were fading into the background and the company went on to become one of the great financial institutions of North America.

Crossing of the Red River was fixed at Winnipeg so that there was an initial 'big curve' in the line as it looped around from the town of Selkirk. Eventually a direct line to the east was constructed (and is in use today) but the original line gave, in effect, a double track from Winnipeg to Molson, thirty-eight miles to the east. Van Horne directed that the line to the west should go straight from Winnipeg to the Pacific coast by the shortest possible route. This resulted in a line generally well to the south of that laid out by Sandford Fleming, going through what were to become the cities of Regina and Calgary, thence into the mountains up the valley of the Bow River. This prairie section of the Canadian Pacific was not, as is often imagined, across flat plains giving easy construction. It was, rather, over the low rolling hills of the prairies that Canadians know so well, with many obstacles in the way of laying a well-graded railway line, but obstacles that were minor in comparison with those to be faced to the east and to the west of this long central portion of the CPR. Men, supplies and horses and scrapers were poured in to keep the work going at top speed. Winnipeg was the main supply point, materials coming up from the USA, rails from England being even shipped to New Orleans and up the Mississippi River; lumber was brought in from Minnesota and ties from eastern Canada. Supply trains from the central distributing yards in Winnipeg left on regular schedules, a procedure that would today be regarded as almost commonplace, each with enough material for one complete mile of track, but in the 1880s and in the almost untouched country of the west it was clear indication of the organisational genius of Van Horne.

He had promised the board of directors that 500 miles would be built in 1882; 417 miles of main-line track were actually completed with twenty-eight more miles of sidings, a

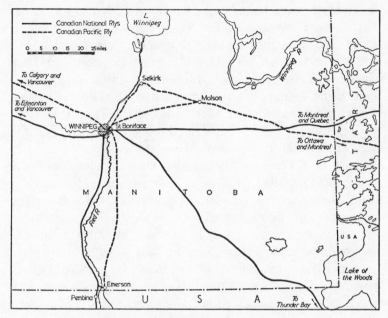

Map E: Main lines serving Winnipeg

truly phenomenal achievement. Over 5,000 men were now at work, night shifts were put on bridge construction, and all this in virgin country, supplies coming up from Winnipeg over a steadily increasing length of completed line. By the summer of 1883 the main line had reached the summit of the Rockies. Here the Kicking Horse Pass was used even though this meant the use of heavy grades for more than twenty miles up to the summit at Hector, followed by an incredibly steep descent to the flats of the Kicking Horse River, at what is now the divisional point of Field. (Picture, p 90.) It must have been realised that the use of this route would result in heavy operating costs as compared with the easy gradients on the route through the Yellowhead Pass two hundred miles to the north, but the proximity to the US border weighed more heavily with the directors and so the CPR was committed to some of the heaviest railroad operating problems of western North America. Magnificent scenery, and such splendid (modern) resorts as

Banff Springs and Lake Louise, would be more than compensation for the travellers of the future but would repay only a small part of the inescapable high operating expenses.

Meantime, work on the difficult section north of Lake Superior finally got started, the route along the shore of the lake being adopted as recommended by Sandford Fleming. The original charter specified that the Canadian Pacific Railway proper should start at Nipissing Junction (Callander) at the east end of Lake Nipissing. Work started here in the late summer of 1882, the first locomotive entering what is now the town of North Bay (that owes its existence to the railway) on 9 November of that year. This stretch of over 600 miles presented formidable obstacles to the contractors since there was no access except by way of the lake, by water in summer and over the ice in winter. Supplies were brought in by water to the extent that was possible, using Owen Sound (near Collingwood) as the main supply port and temporary unloading facilities at convenient points along the inhospitable north shore of the great lake. Much rock excavation was involved. As one travels over this most beautiful route today it is all too easy to forget the quite incredible amount of human endeavour that went into the hand-drilling of holes, the blasting and mucking of the rock in all the many cuts that now look almost as if they were natural features.

In 1883, 100 miles were completed to the west from Callander and thirty-five miles to the east from Fort William. By 1884 track had been laid for 403 out of the 657 miles between Callander and the head of the lake, with 193 additional miles graded. Rail laying was essentially complete by May of 1885. Some 12,000 men and 5,000 horses were employed, twelve steamboats of various sizes were in service for bringing up supplies, and over one million dollars worth of dynamite was used. The worst problems were with the many muskegs, one stretch of track having to be relaid seven times until it was stabilised.

Just as the work was approaching completion, the second Riel Rebellion broke out in the prairies, and for its suppression

Page 89. Mixed steam train on the 3ft 0in gauge White Pass & Yukon Railway on the descent to sea level at Skagway, Alaska, where the grade averages 2-6 per cent for twenty miles

Page 90. Canadian Pacific east-bound transcontinental train from Vancouver to Montreal–Toronto starting its climb up the 'Big Hill' from Field, B.C., headed by one of the famous 2–10–4 Selkirks, No 5929

the Minister of Militia ordered General Middleton to proceed with the necessary troops to the 'Northwest' (as it was still known). Van Horne happened to be in Ottawa at the time, and undertook to deliver the troops to Fort Qu'Appelle over the incomplete track in eleven days if the company were given complete control over all movements. He was relying on his experience with troop movements during the course of the American Civil War. His offer was accepted, and within two days the first two batteries were on their way, arriving in Winnipeg only four days after leaving Ottawa. Lt-Colonel Montizambert, in command of the Artillery, later reported that, 'About 400 miles between the west end of the track and Red Rock or Nepigon—sixty-six miles from Port Arthur— had to be passed by a constantly varying process of embarking and disembarking guns and stores from flat cars to country team sleighs and vice versa. There were sixteen operations of this nature in cold weather and deep snow.' Transport for much of the way was in open flat cars; one report said that eighty miles were traversed in this way with the temperature 50° below zero (F). The completion of this monumental task made a great impression in official and business circles— though it must have been a most trying experience for the troops concerned—and assisted Sir John A. Macdonald in winning essential support in the House of Commons.

The troops were of great service in dealing with the uprising but they had to be reinforced. The first through train between Montreal and Winnipeg brought out 299 men of the Montreal Garrison Artillery. It left Montreal on 11 May 1885, arriving in Winnipeg on 20 May. The time taken is some indication of the difficulties of the journey since this really was the first train to get through and not the first regular scheduled train. Five days were taken to reach Heron Bay, the first point of contact with Lake Superior. It was decided that, instead of detraining, the troops should wait until the almost completed track was finished. Colonel Oswald of the Montreal Light Infantry, therefore, had the unexpected honour of driving the last spike on the Lake Superior section of the CPR on 16 May

1885. The special train then continued but soon came to a high wooden trestle bridge that had not yet been tested. The engine crew were willing to take the train over if all passengers disembarked. The troops therefore marched over the big bridge, followed by the slowly moving little train. All went well, however, and after similar construction delays the train eventually reached Winnipeg. It was not until 1 November of the same year that regular train service started between Montreal and Winnipeg.

This difficult work north of Lake Superior did not in any way interfere with steady progress in the west. On 4 April of this same climactic year (1885) regular passenger service was inaugurated between Winnipeg and Moose Jaw, then in the Northwest Territories, now in the province of Saskatchewan. In the mountains, track construction had proceeded up and over Rogers' Pass, then down the spectacular valley of the Illecillewaet River, past Revelstoke, crossing the Columbia River towards Eagle Pass. Government construction was still proceeding eastwards from the coast under the contract let to Andrew Onderdonck. The first locomotive had been delivered as early as 1881, coming by sea to Vancouver and then up the Fraser River, where it was landed to assist with construction. Onderdonck completed his contract to Savona's Ferry on 29 July; a month later, the Marquis of Lansdowne, Governor-General of Canada, travelled on this line to a point within twenty-eight miles of the railroad coming from the east. A pleasant spot by the side of a running stream, in Eagle Pass, was chosen for the historic joining of rails from east and west. It was named Craigellachie, the Gaelic name of a famous rock in the valley of the Spey, in Scotland, so well known to Highland Scots that it was used in one of the coded messages sent from London by George Stephen to Donald Smith in Montreal when financial worries were at their worst ('Stand fast, Craigellachie' were the words). A silver spike had been suggested by Donald Smith for the use of the Governor-General but in his unavoidable absence it was Donald Smith himself who had the honour of completing this great project, with a plain iron spike which Van Horne had meanwhile decided to substitute.

The event took place on 7 November 1885 and Major Rogers held the spike for Donald Smith to drive. Among the special company standing around was Sandford Fleming, his square beard making him readily distinguishable in the famous photograph that recorded the great occasion. Van Horne spoke the only 'official' words: 'All I can say is that the work has been well done in every way.' After the shouting and cheering had died down, and the congratulations had been exchanged, the conductor of the special train was reputed, apocryphally, to have added to the piquancy of the scene by shouting 'All aboard for the Pacific'! The special train moved off to the west, arriving at Port Moody on Burrard Inlet on the Pacific coast next day. There was much still to be done before the long track was ready for regular service but on 28 June 1886 the first through train left the old Dalhousie Square Station in Montreal for Port Moody and this great transcontinental service has continued without a break (except during strikes) ever since. Although eventually there would be comparable trans-mountain lines in the United States, a regular passenger service from the shore of the Atlantic, as the harbour of Montreal is, to the Pacific coast was never operated south of the border. Transfers were always necessary at Chicago, such were the complications of US railroading.

Completion of the unbroken rail link of 2,893 miles between Montreal and the Pacific coast was far more than merely the end of a stupendous construction job. In a very real way it gave life to the concept of the 'Dominion from sea to sea', this splendid phrase coming from the eighth verse of the seventy-second Psalm, although this fact is but little appreciated by Canadians of today. Almost immediately, settlement along the track began, soon spreading out on both sides.

British Columbia at last began to feel that it was a part of Canada. These long-term objectives were probably unclear at the time for there were initial difficulties to clear up, one of the most serious being the claim by the CPR against the government for no less than twelve million dollars on the grounds that the government-built section of the road they had taken over was not up to the requisite standards. Arbitration proceedings were initated and dragged on until October 1891 when the CPR were awarded the sum of $579,255 in full payment for any deficiencies in the work they had taken over.

In the east, a good start was made at buying up connecting lines to give necessary rail connections for the main line, especially into the Toronto district. The 'short line' to New Brunswick (page 59) was also built, the CPR leasing or building a series of small lines running east from Montreal to Mattawamkeag in Maine through the Atlantic & North-west Co, and also the New Brunswick system of railways, giving them access to Saint John. George Stephen alleged that he was forced into this step in order to win support for some of the CPR financing and that it was expected that the line would take over Maritime traffic from the ICR which would revert to branch-line status. This never did happen and so there started the keen and healthy rivalry between Saint John, the CPR port, and Halifax, the ICR and later the CNR port, that continues to this day. It would be twenty years before the CPR gained direct access to the port of Halifax, and then only by leasing a road on the north shore of Nova Scotia, necessitating a ferry service across the Bay of Fundy. For some years CPR trains operated into Halifax from Saint John through Moncton and over the rails of the ICR.

The subsequent history of the Canadian Pacific will be considered in a later context but it should here be noted that, with Van Horne's continuing drive, the company pursued an aggressive commercial policy from the start. George Stephen, who had been made a baronet in 1886, retired from the presidency of the company in 1886 with the great task completed; he retired to England and was made a peer in 1891, taking the title Baron Mount Stephen. He died in 1921. Van Horne had been made vice-president of the company in 1884 and succeeded Stephen as president in 1888. Before his retirement, he had selected Thomas Shaughnessy as his successor.

All three men lived to see their early faith fully justified and the Canadian Pacific Railway achieve international fame as the 'world's greatest travel system', with a splendid service throughout Canada. They saw, too, CPR steamship lines operating on both the Atlantic and Pacific and the house flag of the company—designed by Sir William Van Horne—become almost as well known as many national flags.

CHAPTER 7

Branch and Other Lines: 1882-1905

It is now necessary to get an over-view of the railway situation in Canada and this can readily be done by examining the graphical record of the steady growth of finished railway lines in Canada presented in Fig 1. (The statistics from which this record was prepared are given in Appendix 1.) The generally orderly pattern of development is clearly evident— the slow start up to about 1870, then the four decades of regular sustained growth, followed by a remarkable upsurge between 1910 and 1915; then a gradual slowing up until the thirties after which the total length has remained sensibly constant, the length of lines abandoned being compensated for by the new lines that have been built. To many it will be surprising to find no indication in this graph of the building of either the ICR or of the CPR. The romance and glamour attached to the building of these two great lines, and especially of the CPR, has given a very distorted view in the public mind of their significance in the general Canadian railway scene. Of their political importance there is no doubt; they provided the original sinews that tied together the great land mass of Canada, assisting immeasurably in its integration into the modern nation. They still remain vital national rail links even though now duplicated by other lines. But in the overall picture, they represented just so many more miles to be added to the steadily increasing total for the country as a whole.

The totals shown are for single-line track ('single length of road is based' being the official explanation). This presents an almost completely correct picture of Canadian railways,

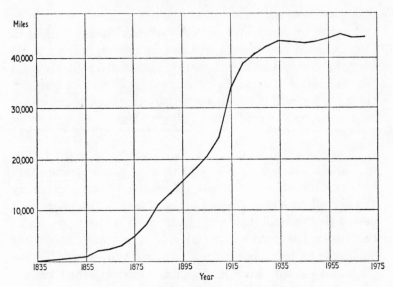

Fig 1: The growth of railway lines in Canada

however, since one of their most surprising features to the interested visitor is that, even today, almost all main lines, and naturally all branch lines, are still single track. The only significant lengths of double-track main line are the 509 miles between Montreal, Toronto and Sarnia (CNR); Montreal, Smith's Falls and Glen Tay, 135 miles (CPR); and the 420 miles from Winnipeg to Fort William on the CPR, this stretch having been necessary for the movement of grain from the prairies to the Lakehead. There are some locations where alternative routes provide the equivalent of double-track service but their length is not very great in the overall total. Around major cities there are naturally sections of multiple track, especially in the vicinity of the great freight marshalling yards which are so important a part of the general scene, but the 'railways' that one thinks of when considering in a general way the rail services in any country are, in Canada, almost entirely single track. Passing loops are, therefore, strategically placed on all lines, at stations when this is convenient, but frequently at locations far from any settlement. The distances between major stations that have already been mentioned will help to make clear the fact that, even today, there are many stations in Canada the only access to which is by rail, the nearest roads being far away. And these isolated stations differ greatly from the stations of Europe, being often only small wooden huts close by the service buildings used by the track maintenance men who are frequently the only residents for many miles around.

New towns had to be created in 'the bush' (as the forests of Canada are usually known) when divisional points were necessary for major servicing of locomotives. Located generally at intervals of about 150 miles, these railway towns came to have a character all their own. In the long stretch from North Bay to the Lakehead—over 600 miles of country that is still 'undeveloped' being mainly forest, streams, muskegs and lakes— the railway towns were the original settlements and remain important but still relatively isolated settlements. Road construction, stemming from the completion of the Trans-Canada Highway in 1962, is gradually reducing the isolation of many railway communities but there remain a great number of faithful Canadian railway workers who live far removed from all the pleasures of urban living. One of the many special services for such Canadians has been the operation of travelling 'school cars' which would remain parked on spurs adjacent to very small isolated railway communities so that the children could have the benefit of personal teaching from regular teachers, supplementing at intervals the continuing efforts of their parents.

Another general feature of railways in Canada that has added to the cost and problems of operation from the earliest days is the necessary provision of train ferry services. About 15 per cent of the total land area of Canada, the second largest country of the world it is useful to remember, consists of islands, and to their residents communication with the mainland is vital. Railways have played their part well and still perform a great service in this special way, despite the advent of automotive transport. Newfoundland does not loom large in this picture, not because it only joined Canada as the tenth province in 1949 but because the Newfoundland Railway, now part of Canadian National Railways, is narrow gauge so that only limited transfer of equipment from the mainland of Canada has been called for. Some standard-gauge rolling stock is now accommodated on special narrow-gauge tracks, and containers are regularly interchanged. A splendid ferry service, with connecting trains, has long been provided between North Sydney, on Cape Breton Island in Nova Scotia, and Port aux Basques at the south-western tip of Newfoundland, the usual journey being an overnight trip by boat, indicative of the length of even this crossing.

Trains to Cape Breton Island, with its active coalmines and steelworks in the Sydney area and access to the ferry service to Newfoundland, come off the main CNR line at Truro. Until 1955 they ran as far as Mulgrave on the narrow tide-swept Strait of Canso across which operated a fleet of strong ice-breaking train ferries, connecting with the Cape Breton lines at Port Hawkesbury. The crossing, though a short one of only two miles, could be difficult, especially in winter, and for many years, there was strong agitation to have a permanent crossing constructed. A bridge was proposed and could have been constructed but the final solution, completed in 1955, was the building of a large rock-fill causeway including a big navigation lock for ocean vessels passing through the strait. A CNR line runs across the top of this great causeway, giving direct service to Cape Breton and eliminating all delays. An interesting by-product has been the development of one of the greatest deep-water ports of the world, with depths up to 100 ft only 750 ft from shore, in the seven miles of the strait now sheltered by the rock-fill crossing.

Prince Edward Island, therefore, now provides the major example of train ferry service in eastern Canada. Separated by Northumberland Strait from the mainland, The Island has had the question of crossing to the mainland as one of its major political problems for over a century. The seven miles at the narrowest crossing do not involve much deep water so

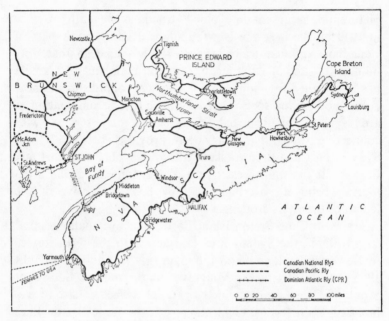

Map F: Railways in the Maritime Provinces

that there have been continuing discussions, and political promises, of building a bridge-tunnel permanent crossing. Economic studies make this quite improbable and so The Island continues to be served by one of the finest train ferry services of North America. Trains leave the main CNR line at Sackville and run to Cape Tormentine, whence the ferries operate to Borden, on The Island. In the great days of rail travel, daily sleeping-car service was available from Charlottetown, capital of the province, to Montreal as also from Cape Breton, transfer of the sleeping cars to the ferry vessels being always a matter of interest to travellers. Freight cars only are now transferred, the current problem being the provision in summertime of enough accommodation for the transfer of the ubiquitous automobiles and caravans that cross to The Island in their thousands.

On the West Coast, transfer of freight cars between the mainland at Vancouver and Vancouver Island, on which the capital city of British Columbia is situated, has long been an efficient tug and barge operation. The length of the crossings to the island is such that passenger traffic has always been taken care of by regular passenger vessels. From Prince Rupert there is even operated a freight car-ferry service to the small town of Ketchikan in Alaska, USA, pulp and paper products from a completely isolated plant there being loaded in freight cars, brought by barge to Prince Rupert, and only then put on the rails of a railway proper, to travel over CNR tracks into the United States. This is only one, even though perhaps the most unusual, of the several international train-ferry connections between Canada and the United States. The original connection between Prescott and Ogdensburg (the 'h' has long since been dropped) continued as a CPR service across the St Lawrence until 1971. For many years there was a busy service across Lake Ontario from Cobourg (CNR) to Rochester (NYCRR) and through the years there have been a number of these cross-lake services, all for freight traffic, supplementing the normal interchanges at border points on land. Coal from the mines of Pennsylvania was at one time a major item in this international traffic until generally displaced by oil.

Most of these services were well developed by the close of the nineteenth century, part of the steady development of the rail system of eastern Canada as it is known today. The GTR continued to provide the principal service from Montreal to Toronto. Competition in western Ontario with the GWR led to many difficulties and much public dissatisfaction; eventually the GTR bought out its rival, amalgamation taking place on 12 August 1882. Two years later, it absorbed the Midland Railway, an aggregation of small Ontario branch lines, 450 miles in total length. Connection with the United States across the St Clair River at Sarnia gradually became a difficult operating problem, despite good train-ferry service, and it was decided to form a permanent crossing by means of a tunnel. This was a bold step since underwater tunnelling was still in its infancy. Work started on 1 January 1889 and the bore was completed on 24 August 1890. An engine and one car passed through on 9 April 1891 but the official opening took place only on 19 September of that year. Connecting Sarnia with Port Huron in Michigan, the tunnel is 20 ft in diameter so that it could accommodate double track although with some clearance limitations in recent years: it has now only a single track. Driven through the local blue clay, it is lined with cast-iron segments and has performed well. (Picture, p 143.)

Operations were at first with steam locomotives, a specially powerful design being developed with Baldwin's of Philadelphia for tackling the gradients at the tunnel approaches. Of 0—10—0 type, they were believed to be the largest in the world at the time, weighing 200,000 lb. Ventilation proved to be a problem and so electrical operation was instituted in 1906, continuing until the advent of the diesel-electric locomotive. The opening of the St Clair tunnel naturally revolutionised the service between Montreal, Toronto and Chicago and this soon became one of the very heavily travelled routes of eastern North America. Inevitable was the doubling of this important main line; this was started at the Montreal end in 1888, finished as far as Toronto by 1903, and to Sarnia by 1905. Through sleeping-car service was initiated between Montreal and Chicago in 1891; named trains (such as the International Limited) soon made the Montreal-Toronto-Chicago service favourably known far beyond Canadian borders. Only in 1970 were sleeping cars between Toronto and Chicago withdrawn as a part of the so-called 'rationalisation' of North American passenger rail service.

Branch lines slowly developed to add their own peculiar flavour to Canadian rail travel, and to feed the main lines with much needed traffic. In Cape Breton Island and the neighbouring part of mainland Nova Scotia, a number of short lines were constructed to serve the growing number of coalmines. The south shore of the beautiful Gaspé Peninsula, long settled by fishermen and notable for the lovely harbour at the town of Gaspé, attracted railway enthusiasts. Those were the days when ocean terminals were being dreamed of in the most unlikely places, and Gaspé was contemplated as a great ocean port. Two separate railways were incorporated, each starting at the small town of New Carlisle, one eastwards to Gaspé, the other westwards to join with the Intercolonial at Matapedia Junction. The names given to them were perhaps their most unusual feature. The Atlantic, Quebec & Western displayed the hopes of those responsible for the line connecting New Carlisle with Gaspé. The Atlantic & Lake Superior showed even more splendid dreams on the part of the promoters of the western line, even this grandiloquent name being changed later to the Quebec Oriental! The combined length of the two connecting lines is only 202 miles, but they remained separate entities until absorbed into the CNR system in 1929.

Strange though the Gaspé story may seem, it is a mere commonplace when compared with a railway development of the eighties near Montreal. The provincial government of Quebec engaged, for a time, in an extensive programme of railway building north of the island of Montreal. The Quebec, Montreal, Ottawa & Occidental Railway (QMOOR) was one of its creations, running on the north shore of the Ottawa and St Lawrence rivers. Well built and operated, the line suffered from the fact that it had no connection with any other railway. The GTR were determined that it should not, this being one of the reasons leading to its purchase of the Midland Railway, when a link with the QMOOR appeared to be a possibility. Although the latter had its own line on the island of Montreal, it could not make connection with the railways on the south shore of the St Lawrence since the GTR owned the only crossing, the Victoria Bridge. The South Eastern Railway (a regional line which connected with a line to Boston) on the other hand, had its terminus at St Lambert on the south shore but could not reach Montreal. The two lines decided to join forces. Rails were laid to the banks of the St Lawrence, downstream of the Victoria Bridge, at Hochelaga and Longueuil respectively, and a large train ferry was purchased to provide the connection between the two railways. 'La Compagnie du

Traverse de chemin de fer d'Hochelaga à Longeuil' was organised to operate the train ferry and to provide also a winter crossing. This was the famous 'Montreal Ice Railway'.

Despite much unfavourable advance comment, arrangements were made to lay a standard railway track on the solid ice of the River St Lawrence in January 1880, preliminary borings having shown the ice thickness to vary from 24 to 48 in. Timbers, 12 in × 12 in, were laid in crib-like formation to spread the load and on top of them standard ties were laid, to which were spiked lightweight iron rails. The line was completed from Longeuil to Hochelaga by 28 January and on that date loaded cars were hauled, by horses, from the south shore to the island of Montreal. The official opening took place on 31 January when a small locomotive (the *W. H. Pangman*) hauled two flat cars, equipped with seats for the many distinguished visitors, safely across the ice. The locomotive weighed 25 tons, the two cars about 8 tons each so that, with 250 passengers, the total load was about 60 tons. The ice railway was used, safely, until the end of March, the train ferry being able to take up its sailings again in mid-April. The same pattern was repeated during the next three winters but with the sale of the North Shore Railway and later of the South Eastern Railway to the CPR, better counsels prevailed and the necessity for this strange crossing disappeared. From its formation until its own bridge across the St Lawrence was completed in 1887, the CPR used the GTR's Bonaventure Station in Montreal, a strange premonition of the enforced cooperation of CNR and CPR that was to come fifty years later.

Branch lines spread out from Montreal, as from the other growing cities, not exactly as suburban lines, for the cities themselves were still metropolitan centres in embryo, but generally to connect smaller towns with the main centres. Occasionally there were other reasons. Typical was the line from Montreal north-west to Lac Remi in the Laurentian Mountains (part of the same Precambrian Shield that was such a formidable barrier to the CPR). The Laurentians come within forty miles of Montreal; for long they remained as forest country with a minimum of settlement. Then a truly pioneering priest, Curé Labelle, started a colonisation movement for these and similar areas. Roads were non-existent and so railways were needed for settlement. The Montfort Colonisation Railway was built in 1893 as a narrow-gauge line, with a standard-gauge connection to Montreal; its name was changed in 1898 to the Montfort & Gatineau Colonization Railway Co, indicative of yet another unrealised railway dream. Together with other rural Laurentian branches running generally northward from Montreal, the Montfort-Lac Remi line came within a few miles of the Gatineau River valley running north from Ottawa, in which a branch line was built in the 1890s. Connection between the two systems was 'obvious' on a map but difficult of execution; the link was never made and traffic on the branch lines has now faded. In the case of the Lac Remi line, the end came with great suddeness. The Quebec Government built the first of its 'autoroutes', or toll-roads close to the line. Traffic had never been heavy, even after it was converted to standard gauge and had become part of the CNR system. After due public hearings, the line was closed in 1963 and shortly thereafter dismantled. In the meantime, the Laurentian area and the Gatineau valley have become famous as ski-resorts, weekend traffic being of phenomenal proportions but the 'ski-specials' of earlier days are no more, the automobile having taken over completely.

The line up the Gatineau valley from Ottawa extends to Maniwaki, eighty-two miles to the north, through well forested and beautiful country. It has always been an important transporter of wood and wood products, this being its only traffic today, apart from 'way-freight', since passenger service was discontinued in 1963. Starting originally on the north shore of the Ottawa River, it gained access to Ottawa (on the south shore) only in 1900 when the Interprovincial Bridge across the Ottawa was completed. When built, this cantilever steel bridge was the longest of its kind in North America, with a main span of 1,050 ft. It is still in service although now carrying automobiles only.

Railways had pushed their way in the eighties up the Ottawa River valley from the vicinity of Montreal, one being purchased by the CPR to form a connection between Callander and Montreal. Running over the flat plain of the St Lawrence, they were not unusual lines. Quite different were the lines built for carrying lumber from the forests to the American market. One of these lines was also unusual in that it was financed privately by one of the great men of the early lumber trade, John Rudolphus Booth. In 1883 he completed, as his own line, the Canada Atlantic Railway (CAR) between Ottawa and Coteau, on the St Lawrence, forty miles west of Montreal, where a train-ferry river crossing gave direct access to the adjoining USA. A passenger service from Montreal was established using this line, the start of the CNR Ottawa-Montreal service of today. Three high-speed 4—4—2 locomotives were purchased from Baldwin's (with Vauclain compound cylinder arrangement), one of them having $84\frac{1}{4}$ in diameter driving wheels, the all-time record for Canada. Once this basic service was operating, J. R. Booth (as he was always known) turned his attention to the prime purpose of the line; he planned and constructed a western extension through the forests of what is now Algonquin Provincial Park (a protected area of over 3,000 square miles) as far as Depot Harbour on Georgian Bay, Lake Huron. Total length from Depot Harbour to the US border at East Alburgh, Vermont, was 396.6 miles. The extension was built first as two lines; these were then amalgamated into the Ottawa, Arnprior & Parry Sound Railway; this, in turn, was absorbed in 1899 into the parent CAR.

It was a tough line to operate. From a station called Killaloe, there was a seven-mile stretch with a 1 per cent grade, summit level being 1,605 ft above sea level. A stud of powerful 2—8—0s were purchased from Baldwins, also Vauclain compounds, and they provided the motive power. Madawaska, a small settlement about midway from Ottawa to Parry Sound (Depot Harbour) was the divisional point equipped wih a five-stall roundhouse and other railway

Page 107. (Above) *Winter scene at Matapedia Junction, Quebec, on the* CNR *main line in 1935, with Ocean Limited on the left and Gaspé branchline train on the right;* (below) CPR *Pacific No 2373 taking over westbound transcontinental train to Vancouver from diesel units at Kamloops, B.C., in 1954, during long-distance trials of diesel units*

Page 108. (Above) CNR *commuter train from Vaudreuil to Montreal hauled by one of the several 4–6–4 well tanks specially designed for this service;* (below) CNR *day train eastbound from Toronto to Montreal, hauled by No 5700, one of several 4–6–4s designed for this route*

facilities. The extension to Georgian Bay was intended to attract some of the grain trade; grain elevators were built at the water's edge. These hopes did not materialise and even the hauling of lumber on the line did not fulfill expectations with the result that the Booth family sold the entire system to the GTR in 1905. Operations continued until 1933 when a beaver dam caused so serious a flood near the track that a section was washed out some distance to the west of Madawaska, in what is now Algonquin Park. Beaver dams, frequently found in the Shield country, have been a constant source of worry in maintaining a number of eastern Canadian lines. The dams can be removed by blasting but, if the location is favoured by the beavers, it is not uncommon for a new dam to be completed within a day or two. The break in the CAR was the beginning of the end for its western section. Progressive closures followed, all lines to the west of Scotia Junction being closed in 1955. That part of the line from Ottawa to Barry's Bay continued in operation until 1961; today it is open for freight service only. The old right of way through 'The Park' has become overgrown, the roundhouse and other railway buildings at Madawaska being recognisable now only as ruins in a woodland glade.

Beyond the Ottawa valley came the 'thousand-mile gap' across the Precambrian Shield before the prairies were reached. The significance in the history of Canadian railways of this long section of essential railway without any appreciable local traffic cannot be over-emphasised. It would be the mid-twentieth century before any large industrial plants were to be found in this wild area, apart only from the modest earlier developments around the Lakehead, originally the twin cities of Fort William and Port Arthur but, since 1970, the united city of Thunder Bay. In the closing years of the last century, therefore, it was to the prairies that one had to look for the next signs of railway development. Branch-line construction started early. Wheat farming as the great industry of the west depended entirely upon adequate transportation. So started the network of branch lines, initially feeding into the

CPR main line, that would eventually cover the three prairie provinces. The familiar sight of the straight single track, the cluster of small buildings around a solitary railway station, all dominated by the gaunt beauty of the standard grain elevator, was soon to be repeated throughout the West. And it was one such small prairie line that was to be the start of the next major development in the history of the railways of Canada.

CHAPTER 8

Canadian Northern Railway: 1896-1917

In 1896 the long reign of the Conservative government came to an end. Apart from the five years of Liberal administration, from 1873 to 1878, the Conservatives had been responsible for these three critical formative decades of the new nation. Until his death in 1891, Sir John A. Macdonald had given the country outstanding leadership. Four men subsequently served as Prime Ministers in the five years prior to the general election of 1896 so that it was not surprising, perhaps, that the Liberal party won, assuming office on 11 July 1896. Sir Wilfrid Laurier, another of the great men of early Canada, became Prime Minister and so served for the next fifteen years, until defeated in the critical 'Reciprocity Election' of 1911. The Liberals were fortunate, since the closing years of the century saw the start of a period of real prosperity, following the lean years of the previous decade. They truly rode on the crest of the wave; railway building came to be a principal beneficiary.

Some indication of the times is given by the overall immigration picture. Despite the valiant efforts of the Government of Canada and of the CPR in trying to attract settlers to the western plains, immigration dropped to a record low of 16,855 in 1896. Emigration to the United States left a negative balance until 1901 but then the great flood of new citizens from Europe really started, the rate of growth in total population in the first decade of the new century (35 per cent) being higher than for any other country of the world. In 1913 no less

111

than 200,000 persons came to Canada to make it their home. New capital followed the settlers, two and a half billion dollars being invested in Canada between 1910 and 1913, 70 per cent of this coming from Great Britain (in such great contrast to recent trends).

The times were therefore ripe for adventurous spirits. In William Mackenzie and Donald Mann, Canada found two men who were to achieve spectacular success in railroad building. Mackenzie had been a small-town teacher who kept a country store. Mann was intended for the ministry but turned instead to construction, becoming a foreman. They both worked on the building of the CPR, later coming together and forming a partnership so effective that 'Mackenzie and Mann' is still a term of meaning in the Canada of today. In 1896, they acquired the charter of the Lake Manitoba Railway & Canal Co which had been granted in 1889 to provide for a line north of the CPR into north-western Manitoba and on to tidewater on Hudson Bay. The venture was not successful until the partners took it over. In their first year they completed eighty-five miles of track and ran the first train from Gladstone to Dauphin, two very small places just to the west of Lake Manitoba, on 15 December 1896. Regular operation started early in 1897. The line was extended northward to Winnipegosis, on the lake of that name; running powers were obtained from Gladstone southwards into Portage La Prairie (on the CPR) over the rails of the Manitoba North-Western Railway. Mixed trains were operated twice a week using second-hand or borrowed stock; it was said that the entire line was operated by thirteen men and a boy and this may well have been the case, so frugal were the partners and so lightly settled the country served by the line.

The hidden factor in this simple beginning of one of the truly great railway stories of North America was the existence in the original charter of provision for a federal government land grant of 6,000 acres of land per mile up to a total length of 125 miles. To this the provincial government added a guarantee of bonds up to $8,000 per mile for the same distance.

After reaching Winnipegosis, which in those days must have been truly the 'end of the world' apart only from travel on the adjoining great lake and river system, the partners gave up any idea of building on to Hudson's Bay and turned their attention to more lucrative areas. In 1901, the Canadian Northern Railway (CNOR, the new name having been adopted in 1899) took over from the provincial government the small lines that it then owned, by default or purchase, totalling 350 miles in length, giving it a connection to Winnipeg and including the valuable branch line to Pembina on the US border where connection was made with the rail system of the States. Mackenzie and Mann then started construction of another southward trending line, the Manitoba & Southeastern Railway running initially from St Boniface (across the Red River from Winnipeg) to Marchand, well on the way to another US border point at the extreme south-east corner of the province. The first forty-five miles of this line to be completed paid its way by the haulage of firewood to the urban Winnipeg area, sure indication of the still developing state of the new settlements. By 1902, they had reached Port Arthur through the acquisition of small lines and by additional construction under the Manitoba & Southeastern charter.

Already Mackenzie and Mann had entered eastern Canada by the purchase in 1901 of a three-mile line from Parry Sound to a connection with the CAR, but this was just a beginning. In 1903 the CNOR entered Quebec with the purchase of the Great Northern Railway of Canada, and the Chateauguay & Northern Railway. This gave them access to Montreal, the line thence to Hawkesbury being one-half of what would soon be an alternative route to the CPR line between Montreal and Ottawa. They even purchased a small line on the south shore of Nova Scotia. By the end of the year 1903, the Canadian Northern Railway had a total mileage of 1,706, 344 miles of which were in eastern Canada. In all these and subsequent acquisitions, Mackenzie and Mann were ably assisted by Zebulun Lash who has been described as the 'subtlest framer of legal clauses and monetary expedients in the annals of

Canada'. He was solicitor to Mackenzie & Mann & Co (incorporated in 1902), and a director, holding one qualifying share. Mackenzie and Mann, however, kept the majority interest in the company to themselves, dividing all common stock equally, with what satisfactory results will appear a little later.

The Government of Canada was naturally more than usually interested in all new railway developments, not only because of their financial involvement through continuing grants and bond guarantees, but also because of their concern for the orderly development of the rapidly growing country. The move of the CNOR into eastern Canada was at first frowned upon by the government, Sir Wilfrid Laurier himself attempting to dissuade them from this step. He was not successful. Although nothing was said at the time, it was revealed later (by Sir Donald Mann, both men being knighted) that about 1903 he and his partner had made approaches to the CPR regarding suitable arrangements for extending their service, but without success. The conclusion is inescapable that it must have been at about this time, if not indeed before 1903, that these two energetic men had conceived the idea of a second trans-continental railway in rivalry to the CPR.

They continued their aggressive expansionist policy, always selecting lines where paying business might be immediately expected and where construction was cheap. They were well served by their engineering staff, who kept all construction expenditures to a minimum. By 1905 they had a main line from Winnipeg to Edmonton, and eastwards from Winnipeg to Port Arthur, with some lines to the east of Lake Superior, the 'thousand-mile gap' being still a barrier to their further hopes. Significant, however, is the fact that the company had established its head office in Toronto in 1899. It was not until 1908 that the final step of embarking on surveys for a line through the mountains of the west was taken. Naturally, the early work of Sir Sandford Fleming was used to good effect. The easy route through the Yellowhead Pass was adopted and the decision taken to follow down the Fraser

River to Vancouver. The work was expensive but not difficult in comparison with the earlier building of the CPR. The last spike was driven at Basque, British Columbia, but this was not until September 1915 when the first world war was demanding all public attention so that the event passed with but little notice.

During these same prosperous pre-war years, the gap north of Lake Superior was also bridged. A line had been built up from Toronto to Sudbury in 1908. The long stretch to Port Arthur was located in a great sweep well to the north of the lake, through the bush-river-and-lake country with no prospect of any immediate business but involving easier and therefore more economical construction than the CPR lake-shore line. Freight service was inaugurated between Toronto and Winnipeg in 1915 and some months later passenger service from Quebec to Vancouver was available on this new line that had started so inauspiciously in the backwoods of Manitoba just twenty-five years before. Further developments were taking place in eastern Canada. More lines were acquired in Nova Scotia. Improvements were made to the lines in Quebec, especially around Montreal, leading eventually to the bold decision to create a new terminal in the centre of the expanding city even though this involved the construction of a three-mile tunnel beneath Mount Royal, the splendid mountain that gave the city its name, the slopes of which are still preserved, in the main, as a fine natural park. A double-track tunnel was excavated most fortunately for future traffic, and electrical traction arranged from the 'Tunnel Terminal' (as the new terminal was called) out to the north side of the island of Montreal where steam locomotives took over.

By 1918, CNOR lines extended from coast to coast with a total mileage of over 10,000. Standards of construction were low but good enough for the generally low density of traffic, even though it was said that 'the track had a regrettable tendency to jump up and hit the trains from behind'. The legal complications created by the almost haphazard association of so many small companies were probably only fully understood by

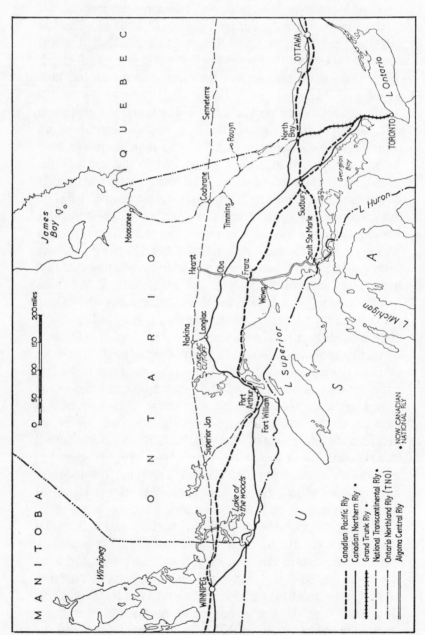

Map G: Canadian railways around the Great Lakes

Zebulun Lash. Financial arrangements were almost as complicated. Cash subsidies had been received from federal, provincial
and municipal governments; land grants had been made and
land sold; loans had been obtained from the Canadian
Government; and there was a wide variety of bonds outstanding, most of them guaranteed by either the federal or provincial
governments. In total, Mackenzie and Mann had been given
seven million acres of land and $30 million in cash. Bond issues
to the amount of $245 million had been guaranteed. And the
common stock of the company, still held by Mackenzie and
Mann, was valued at $58,614,000, of which $51,000,000 was
reported to have been pledged to the Canadian Bank of
Commerce against advances. Other estimates placed the value
of the common stock even higher.

Trouble was in the air, however, as will be clear when the
even more remarkable story of the third transcontinental line
is outlined. In July 1916 a Royal Commission had been
appointed to study transportation in general in Canada, and
in particular the status of the three transcontinental railways.
The commission's report was presented in the spring of 1917,
and in August of that year the government (now again a
Conservative administration) announced that they were
prepared to take over the CNOR. This precipitated a bitter
debate in parliament but the government had its way, and a
board of arbitration was established to determine the payment
that should be made for the outstanding stock. The reports
of this board, and of the experts engaged to examine and value
the property, constitute invaluable railway records of con-
suming interest. The three arbitrators reached a unanimous
conclusion—that the outstanding shares should be valued at
$10,800,000, although they did not disclose how they arrived
at this figure; there was much public criticism of this decision.
The government had already assumed control of the line,
taking it over in September 1917 and appointing a new board
of directors. They charged the restructured company with
responsibility for the management of the already extensive
Canadian Government Railways (including the ICR, always

under government control), and in December authorised the board to use the designation 'Canadian National Railways' for the lines they operated. The final stage in the establishment of CNR, however, had to await the nationalisation of the GTR and Grand Trunk Pacific Railways. To the development of the latter attention must now be directed. As its strange history is told, it will be impossible to avoid wondering what the future of the CNOR might have been if it had not been faced with the recalcitrant opposition of the man responsible for this strangest railway in Canadian history.

CHAPTER 9

Grand Trunk Pacific: 1902-23

The Grand Trunk Railway Co was in the background of all the major developments of Canadian railways in the closing decades of the nineteenth century. The possibility that they might have operated the Intercolonial line from Halifax to Montreal has been mentioned. Rather than this, they sold their own line from Levis to Riviére du Loup to the Government of Canada. Their opposition to the CPR project was understandable, perhaps, but it appears to have influenced public opinion in later years. The company continued to consolidate its lines throughout Ontario, in which province most of its mileage was concentrated, the construction of the St Clair Tunnel (p 101) being indicative of the improvements made in their mainline service. A greatly improved bridge across the Niagara River at Niagara Falls, so vital a connection with US lines, was provided in 1897. During the same period the original tubular superstructure of the Victoria Bridge in Montreal was replaced by stronger steel truss spans. And on 1 May 1899 the GTR assumed control of the Central Vermont Railway (CVR) the main line of which ran from the Canadian border to New London, Connecticut, thus providing another Atlantic port for their overseas traffic. By the end of the century, the GTR system had a total mileage of about 5,000 miles, all of which was in eastern Canada.

Control and ultimate management of the company, however, was still exercised from London, England. Since most of the public investment in the GTR was in the hands of British investors, this situation can be appreciated even though it is now clear that it was not the most satisfactory arrangement. There appeared to be a tendency on the part of the management to listen to the insistent demands of shareholders for the payment of dividends rather than to ensure, through a more prudent use of funds, the necessary maintenance of the property in Canada. The major works just mentioned added to the financial complications, with the result that the company found itself in considerable financial difficulty just as the century came to a close. In order to salvage the situation, the management engaged the services of another US railway man. This was Charles Melville Hays, who first arrived in Canada in 1896 and was fated to be a leading participant in the Canadian railway drama of the next decade.

Hays had achieved spectacular success in rescuing the Wabash Railway from similar difficulties and so he came across the border with high recommendations. He was given, as general manager, the full support of the president and directors and proceeded to do an equally good job on the GTR. After a brief year spent again in the United States, Hays served as general manager of the GTR until 1909, and thereafter as president until 1912, when he was drowned in the loss of the *Titanic*. His activity was early made evident. Running rights were granted to the CPR over the Toronto to Hamilton line; a good rental was also obtained from the Wabash Railway for running powers over 500 miles of GTR track; and the Chicago extension was put into receivership and reorganised as the Grand Trunk Western Railroad (GTWR) with a considerable reduction in interest charges. By 1902 the operating deficit of the years immediately previous had been changed into a good surplus, but demands from shareholders soon used up these satisfactory operating profits.

Hays, however, had his eyes on wider fields of activity. The financial success of the CPR company was public knowledge. The West of Canada was slowly filling up with new settlers. Optimism was in the air as to the future prospects of the Dominion, and Hays was determined not to let slip any further opportunities of sharing in expansionist schemes.

He was able to persuade his management to support the incorporation of a new company known as the Grand Trunk Pacific Railway Co (GTPR), with an authorised capital of $45 million, and the avowed purpose of building yet another trans-continental line in order to give the GTR access to the west and the Pacific. As a single competitor to the CPR, such a venture could be understood but it was already clear that the CNOR also had ideas about a transcontinental line. Efforts were made by the Government of Canada, personally by Sir Wilfrid Laurier, to bring Hayes into agreement with Mackenzie and Mann, but without success. The available records suggest that some effort was made by the GTR authorities to purchase the interest of Mackenzie and Mann in 1902 but no sale was possible, as can well be imagined in view of the pioneering character of the two western partners.

During the winter of 1902–03 meetings were held in Ottawa, at least once in Sir Wilfrid's own office, in an attempt to get the two companies to work together. The proposal that the GTR should provide service in the east of Canada, being connected to the CNOR system in the west, was an eminently sound one. It would have provided suitable competition to the CPR, the country being already prosperous enough, and with enough potential, to support two transcontinental lines—but not three. In the arbitration proceedings of 1918 Sir Donald Mann stated that 'We offered to build a joint section from Port Arthur to North Bay, and we would develop the west and they would develop in the east . . . they refused and would do nothing but buy us out.' All the efforts proved abortive.

Sir Wilfrid Laurier had said publicly: 'I am well aware that this plan (for a *second* transcontinental railway) may scare the timid and frighten the irresolute, but I may claim that every man who has in his bosom a stout Canadian heart will welcome it as worthy of this young nation, for whom a heavy task has no terrors, which has the strength to face grave duties and grave responsibilities.' Sir Wilfrid was a great and wise leader of Canada, but why he did not persist in bringing together the two great projects for a transcontinental rail crossing will probably never be known with certainty. Caught up in the prevailing national spirit of optimism, his espousal of a new railway across the country in such words as have been quoted can be understood—not for nothing had he earned the name of 'the silver-tongued orator'—but how any of his advisers could have been so blind to the financial implications of building *two* new transcontinental lines is now almost impossible to understand, even making every allowance for the benefit of hindsight. The Laurier Government had been spending large sums on canal construction; they were under considerable pressure to build the Georgian Bay ship-canal (up the Ottawa River) which would have given an all-Canadian seaway to the Great Lakes. And yet, despite these and many other vital factors, they gave up trying to bring the CNOR and the GTR together. Not only so, but they signed a contract of a most unusual character with the GTR authorities, as was announced to the public of Canada on 30 July 1903.

Significantly, the announcement came not from the government but from Mr Hayes himself. When, next day, the public clamoured for more information, Hayes was not to be found, having travelled south during the night on his way to an Atlantic crossing to London. When details were revealed, naturally with suggestions that action had to be taken quickly before American competitors gained an advantage over Canada, it was found that the government was undertaking to build a 'National Transcontinental Railway' (NTR) from Moncton (near the border of New Brunswick and Nova Scotia), through Quebec City, and then through the wild country that then existed (and still does to a large extent) all around the direct route from Quebec to Winnipeg. This line would be built by the government and then leased to the GTPR which, in turn, would construct a new railway across the prairies, through the mountains by way of the Yellowhead Pass, and on to a new port on the Pacific at a small coastal town known as Port Simpson. The lease of the NTR to the GTPR included responsibility for operation also, for seven years at no rent, then at 3 per cent of the cost of construction per annum for the remainder of the fifty-year term. Sir Wilfrid's explanation of this most unusual arrangement to the House of Commons was almost as unusual. Debate in the House was bitter and prolonged, but eventually the Liberal administration had its way and Canada was saddled with the prospect of a railway debt that would be an immediate worry to the next generation, and a continuing burden even today.

Not only were the contractural arrangements unusual, but so also was the decision to build a new line through New Brunswick and eastern Quebec that would duplicate the ICR, still operating well but not profitably. And not only was this route chosen but standards of construction were decided upon, apparently in consultation with the GTR, that would be almost as high as any in North America. The enthusiasm and high hopes for the future that these decisions reflect were indicated by the fact that the first offer of bonds for financing the new western line in London, England, was subscribed ten times over. Speeches of the time suggest that some of those responsible still thought that the new line would attract shipments of wheat from the west for transhipment at Halifax. There were already, however, clear indications that wheat shipments would be by water to the maximum extent possible, even though this would involve large storage facilities at transshipment points. The Lakehead (Fort William and Port Arthur) was already destined to be a major transhipment point.

But the promoters had their way. The line was located with no curve greater than four degrees (a radius of 1,433 ft) and no gradient more than 0.4 per cent without the express permission of the chief engineer. In the line as built there was only one major exception to this, a stretch of twenty miles in eastern Canada with a gradient of 1 per cent. In the difficult mountain section, fifteen relatively short tunnels were necessary to get the straightest possible alignment in accordance with the instructions of Hayes. All bridges were constructed of concrete and steel, the economical practice of earlier and other lines of building first in timber for later replacement in steel and concrete when economics permitted this, being a policy completely discarded. It is small wonder that the final cost proved to be $86,000 per mile.

On the credit side, the stupendous task of building a coast to coast railway, 3,543 miles in length, was successfully completed in about eight years even though another penetration of the 400-mile wide mountain barrier was involved, and the initial exploration of much of the country through which the National Transcontinental section was located. The distance from Moncton to Winnipeg, as finally laid out, was 1,801 miles. The survey work was arranged in six major divisions, averaging about 300 miles in length. No aerial surveying was then possible, so that the more than 800 men in the locating teams had to explore on foot, and through most difficult terrain, country for fifty to one hundred miles on either side of the approximate route. This notable piece of exploration was quickly done, however, with the result that the first sod for the National Transcontinental line was turned by Sir Wilfrid Laurier at Fort William on 12 September 1905. That for the GTPR was delayed until 1906, when it was ceremoniously turned at Portage La Prairie, Manitoba. Work was soon in progress on an unprecedented scale right across the country. Twenty-five thousand men were at work at the peak of construction, aided by the beginnings of modern mechanical equipment, but thousands of horses were still necessary for haulage. The official start of construction at Fort William might seem to be strange since the NTR ran in what might be called a 'straight line' from Quebec to Winnipeg and so did not come near Lake Superior. The planners had included, however, a branch line to Fort William from a junction near Sioux Lookout, now known as Superior Junction. The first shipment of grain over this branch, to the lakehead was made in 1910—an omen of the way that wheat would generally travel on its way from the west to Europe.

Starting at Moncton, the line going west immediately left the settled part of New Brunswick, along the coast and major rivers, and plunged into the untouched forest country. The only town of any size that it passed through was Edmunston,

Page 125. *Special* CNR *train to mark the centenary of the opening of Canada's first railway leaving Montreal on 21 July 1936 behind No 6400, first of a new class of streamlined 4–8–4s*

Page 126. CPR *100-car train with multiple diesel haulage in the mountains of British Columbia en route to Vancouver for transhipment of coal to Japan*

and it was then a very small place indeed. Since it was the *National* Transcontinental Railway, it had to be located in Canada and so it wound along the strange northern border of the state of Maine just inside the province of Quebec, at considerable increase in essential distance and with added complications of location. Throughout its length, as far as the crossing of the St Lawrence between Levis and Quebec, it paralleled the Intercolonial and so was a competitor for its terminus-to-terminus traffic but with no possibility of developing any local traffic apart from what little was involved in forest development.

From the start it was realised that crossing the St Lawrence would be a tremendous task and so the government agreed to construct a bridge at Quebec as a separate undertaking, through its own Department of Railways and Canals. A double-tracked bridge was decided upon, yet another indication of the optimism of the times. The story of the Quebec Bridge—for this crossing is *the* Quebec Bridge—is well known. Started in 1906 as a steel cantilever structure of record-breaking span between massive piers on the two banks at a narrow section of the river a few miles upstream of Quebec City, its design proved to be faulty with the result that the incomplete bridge collapsed in August 1907 with tragic loss of life. A new start was made, after the necessary inquiry, in 1910; the suspended span was successfully raised into place in September 1917 and it was officially opened by another Prince of Wales on 22 August 1919, fifty-nine years after the similar opening of the Victoria Bridge at Montreal. The Quebec Bridge has been in successful service ever since, today carrying automobile traffic as well as an appreciable amount of rail traffic, and now duplicated by an adjacent suspension bridge for the rapidly increasing road traffic across the great river.

Once the new railway left the city of Quebec the same pattern of location was repeated, a first-class line built through virgin forest and lake country, the only settlements for a thousand miles being those necessary for railway operation. Even today, although some mining development has led to the construction of some branch lines, with one major paper-mill town sited on the railway, it is still a 'bush line' having attracted relatively little colonisation to the areas it penetrates. Across the prairies there was the inevitable duplication with the CPR and the CNOR lines, duplication that reached its culmination in the Yellowhead Pass. Construction of the two competing lines was almost simultaneous, to such an extent that surveyors for the GTR tried to conceal their intention to use the Yellowhead Pass by very obviously surveying in other possible locations. But the two lines were built, in places so close together that one might have thought that a double-track line was being installed. Hayes had decided that the GTPR should turn to the north beyond the Pass, rather than going south to Vancouver. He selected in October 1906 the location where the fine Pacific port of Prince Rupert now stands; it was then an isolated spot on Kaien Island, only reached by a crossing over the Zanardi Rapids on the Skeena River.

This was another bold decision for here was to be developed a railway terminal and associated town on a rocky coast, 550 miles north of the nearest settlement on the coast from which all supplies would have to be brought. But this job, too, was done, special stern-wheeler steamers being built for transporting supplies almost 200 miles up the Skeena River, down the valley of which this new rail outlet to the Pacific had been located. The first train from Winnipeg to Prince Rupert arrived on 9 April 1914, four months before the out-break of a war in Europe that was to have such profound effect upon all the hopes for the new transcontinental crossing. The NTR section came into operation in June 1915, but the GTPR had operated services between prairie cities as early as 1910. Joint service with the CNOR in Winnipeg at the fine Union Station on Main Street was inaugurated on 3 January 1913. It was later in this same year that the last spike on the NTR had been driven. Far from being a celebration, this was but the signal for the GTPR to advise the government that it refused to honour its contract to take over and operate the line, due to the staggeringly high costs of construction, costs exceeding the original estimate by one hundred million dollars, or 200 per cent. Political influences on contract awards contributed to the excess cost.

This was the beginning of the end. The Royal Commission that was inevitably appointed to inquire into the cost of construction found that neither the GTPR nor the NTR administrations had exercised proper economy in construction, criticising the high standards for track location in particular. Even before this there had been suggestions of political interference in the carrying out of contracts and even of engineering work. Proof could never be produced but a mild sensation was caused in 1909 when the chief engineer of the NTR, who had done such an outstanding job in directing the exploration surveys, resigned on the grounds that his assistant engineers were not carrying out his instructions. There were the usual questions raised about payments for excavation, whether of soil or rock, at significantly differing unit costs, while in addition there was the complication of the undoubted rise in the general level of labour and material costs. And with the start of the first world war in 1914, the London money market disappeared so that almost insuperable difficulties were faced in raising the funds necessary for the completion of the lines.

The Royal Commission of 1916 (p 117) naturally reported on the GTR situation in its over-view of the entire Canadian railway situation. A majority of the commissioners recommended that the Government of Canada should assume control not only of the CNOR but also of the GTR and the GTPR. A. H. Smith, President of the New York Central and Chairman of the Commission, in a minority report, urged that the GTR operate the eastern lines and the CNR all the western lines (excluding, of course, the CPR which, as all the commissioners agreed, could stand on its own feet). The government would then be required to operate only connecting lines if it was not able to have these also operated by private companies. Although the majority recommendation about taking over the CNOR was followed, it was not possible to take the same action with regard to the GTPR because of the involvement of the GTR. Temporary financial arrangements were therefore made while negotiations with the GTR were started, as the Prime Minister advised the House of Commons in May 1918.

This was not Sir Wilfrid Laurier, however, since the Liberals had been defeated in the general election of 1911, just as the railway building was in top gear. The major topic of the hustings was the matter of reciprocity in trade with the United States although the 'railway problem' must have been seen to be in the background. It is not too difficult to imagine the great worries that had to be born by the new leader, Sir Robert Borden, and his Conservative colleagues—the railway problem inherited from the former administration, so many of their fears as expressed in House debates being now realities, as well as all the problems associated with Canada's war effort from 1914 onwards.

Negotiations were still proceeding with the GTR when, in February 1919, the company advised the government that they expected to have to default in March on the interest due in London on their securities. The government refused any further aid and the interest was paid, but the company then advised the government that they would not operate the GTPR after 10 March. Taking this as a threat intended to get the desired loan, the government thereupon placed the GTPR in receivership, under the War Measures Act, and it was so operated from 10 March 1919 until 1 September 1920. It was not until October 1919 that agreement was reached as to the total value for sale of the GTR itself.

The Government of Canada agreed to take over all the capital stock except for an issue of 4 per cent guaranteed stock on which it did, however, agree to pay interest, the value of the stock to be determined by another board of arbitrators. The importance attached to this investigation is shown by the fact that the company was represented by Mr W. H. Taft, former President of the United States; Sir Thomas White (Minister of Finance) represented the government, the chairman being Sir Walter Cassels, a judge of the Exchequer Court.

Despite Hays' dream of a Pacific outlet having led to such difficult problems, as shown by the desire of the GTR to get rid of the GTPR, it was included in the board's considerations. All lines were inspected; much argument was produced. Payment of dividends by the GTR when there were no earnings to support them was fairly definitely proved, even though these same monies should by rights have been used for repayments to the government. The majority of the arbitration board found that the stock had no value but left a final decision to the government; Mr Taft, who was not uncritical of the company, valued the stock at not less than $48 million. The final decision of the government was widely criticised. An appeal was made to the Privy Council but this was refused. Subsequent legal actions, however, taken by holders of some of the shares, continued to be before the courts until almost the outbreak of the second world war. There were many small investors in England who, not knowing the complex background of the arbitration decision, felt keenly about what they thought 'Canada' had done to them; it is for this reason that this summary of the legal and financial aspects of the GTR has been given.

An action of the English board of directors in voting a year's salary to leading officials ($306,000) out of the company's fire insurance fund, and five years' salary to the directors ($167,800) on the day that the shareholders ratified the agreement with the Canadian Government did not help to dispel the acrimony with which the long history of the GTR as a separate entity came to a close. It was a railway that had done much for the development of Canada. It suffered from the problem of short hauls, especially in comparison with the CPR, comparable receipts per ton being $2.44 and $4.81, respectively. It was well operated at the local level but the fact that management remained centred in England was probably at the root of all the major and certainly the final troubles. The visionary concepts of Charles Hays did not help matters and undoubtedly precipitated the final inevitable take-over of the entire property. A temporary board of management of five members, three from the GTR, operated the system until May 1921. It was arranged that the English board should resign in that month; a new Canadian board under the chairmanship of Sir Joseph Flavelle was appointed and the head office moved to Canada. After the dismissal of the appeal to the Privy Council against the arbitration board's decision, consolidation of the GTR system with the existing governmental lines was started. By the end of January 1923, this had been done and the Act, already passed, incorporating Canadian National Railways, came into effect.

CHAPTER 10

Canadian National Railways: 1923-33

Canadian National Railways was born of necessity for reasons of which no Canadian, even the most avid supporters of public ownership, can be proud. It has become one of the great railway systems of the world but its formation was the only possible solution to profound national difficulties in railway financing, resulting from a combination of blind political optimism, inevitable problems of war-time financing, and questionable management of Canada's first great free-enterprise railway. The name was first used when the Government of Canada took over CNOR in 1918. A small board of directors, with Mr D. B. Hanna (formerly general manager of the CNOR) as president, was appointed to administer the property. Management of the existing Canadian Government Railways was entrusted to this same board later in the year. In 1920, the operation of the GTPR added a yet further responsibility for what proved to be the temporary board. The Act constituting the Canadian National Railway Co was passed in 1919 but only proclaimed in January 1923, when the final step was taken of bringing into this congerie of lines the GTR itself. Mr Hanna and his board faced the initial problems. He was an able railroad man and lost no time in tackling the major task of catching up with deferred maintenance. The government provided the necessary funds. With good management and despite all difficulties, the operating deficit (on gross earnings of over $120 million) was reduced in the four-year interregnum from $20 million to just under $10 million.

Political changes added their own peculiar complications

to the picture. The Conservative administration of Sir Robert Borden was changed in the latter part of the war to a Union government. The general election of late 1921 dislodged a short-lived Conservative administration under Mr Arthur Meighen (elected in July 1920); on 29 December 1921 Mr Mackenzie King began his remarkable career of service to Canada as the new Prime Minister of a Liberal government that remained in power, apart from an interesting three-month break in 1926, for the next decade. It was during these critical years that CNR was forged into a unified and efficient railroad system. Its financial problems remained but these did not interfere with the quite outstanding job of organisation and management supervised by the new board of directors that took office in October 1922, planned and executed by the great man who had been recruited for the extremely difficult task of serving as chairman and president. This was Sir Henry Thornton, brought to Canada after distinguished railroad service in both the United States and Great Britain.

The task he faced would have daunted any lesser man. He had to integrate into one unified railway three privately-owned lines that were essentially bankrupt and four railways built and operated by the Canadian Government. In actual fact, this conglomeration actually consisted of no less than 149 separate companies, the financing of which had been achieved by 251 different security issues. Despite the good start made under Mr Hanna's leadership, a tremendous backlog of deferred maintenance remained, while standards of construction for many of the lines had always been so poor that massive rebuilding was another pressing need. Duplications of services, of structures and even of operating lines had to be studied and the duplications eliminated. On top of all this, there was the staggering problem of the financial burden to which CNR was committed from the start. This was the inflexible decision of government, in contrast to the situation in the United States where, at one time, 30 per cent of all railways west of the Mississippi had been in receivership, almost nine hundred million dollars having been removed from the capital structure. Had similarly drastic steps been taken in Canada, the position of CNR would soon have become financially comparable to that of the CPR but the government had decided that the national credit was of paramount importance. The CPR management had naturally offered to take over the management of the lines that made up CNR but this offer was, equally naturally, refused.

Sir Henry Thornton had, therefore, to do the best he could knowing that the financial burden could not be removed but with the assurance that, under the terms of the CNR Act, any deficits would be met out of the government's consolidated revenue fund. Very early in his career with CNR, Sir Henry stated: 'Let it be understood, now and once and for all, that there is to be no political interference direct or indirect in the administration and working of the CNR. . . . The Prime Minister has solemnly assured me that there is to be no political interference and it was on this distinct understanding that I accepted the post. . . .' With this backing, he went to work. He became an almost legendary figure. The writer can confirm one of the legends. One very cold winter's night, in a blinding snowstorm, he had to leave Montreal on the 8.00 pm Ocean Limited express for Halifax. Going up to see the locomotive at the head of the train, as always, he was surprised to find Sir Henry, muffled up in a big fur coat, chatting away with the driver and fireman before they left on their difficult run into the blizzard across the Victoria Bridge and then off to the east. This he was said always to do when he was in Montreal and able to leave his comfortable home on the slope of Mount Royal.

It is small wonder that in every major railway station throughout Canada that is used by CNR trains there will be found today a bronze plaque bearing these words:

In Memory of
Sir Henry Thornton K.B.E.
Chairman and President
Canadian National Railways
1922–1932
Died March 14th 1933
This tablet erected by the Employees
of Canadian National Railways

This tribute, probably unique in the annals of railroading, tells much about the man. Only a brief summary record can be presented of what he did but here are some of the essential steps that led to CNR being the line it is today.

The Prince Edward Island Railway, previously government-owned, had to be rehabilitated and converted from its narrow gauge of 3 ft 6 in to standard gauge. New train ferries had to be provided so that mainland passenger and freight cars could be brought over to The Island. A new passenger station and hotel were constructed at Halifax, implementing part of a major plan for the port development proposed in 1913. Lines around Quebec City had to be rearranged, bridges strengthened and junctions improved in order to link the GTR and NTR lines together; the St Malo shops, at Quebec, erected by the NTR and opened in 1919, were put to active use. In northern Quebec, an important new branch line was built into the Rouyn mining area. In southern Ontario, the old CNOR line from Toronto to Napanee was removed, all traffic being concentrated on the GTR line. Main lines were reballasted and equipped with new and heavier rails with consequent benefit to travel and to maintenance. By 1924, CNR was able to reduce its running time between Montreal and Winnipeg; CPR had to follow suit.

The prairies were interlaced with new branch lines, located to tap new sources of the wheat that was by that time making this part of Canada world famous. A major new bridge, at the small town of Elbow, Saskatchewan, was constructed to give a much improved crossing of the South Saskatchewan River. Indicative of the size of Canadian waterways, even a thousand miles from the sea, is the fact that the Dunblane Bridge is 1,771 ft long between abutments. It gave improved service between Regina and Moose Jaw, on the one hand, and Saskatoon on the other. In Alberta, the first branch lines to the north, in the direction of the Peace River country, were constructed. In the mountains, the rearrangement of tracks begun during the war years was completed, all duplication being eliminated. In 1917, as part of its war effort, the

Government of Canada had arranged (even then!) for the removal of over 100 miles each of GTPR and CNR track, the materials so obtained being sent immediately to France. From Lobstick Junction in Alberta, to Red Pass Junction in British Columbia, there is now one main line where previously there were two; at the latter point the CNR line to Prince Rupert goes off to the northwest and the CNR line to Vancouver to the south west.

In 1927, the culmination of many years planning by a number of companies including CNR was the official opening of the magnificent Toronto Union Station, used by both CNR and CPR. Correspondingly in Montreal a plan had been devised for combining the three main stations now operated by Canadian National into one major terminal, using the old Tunnel Terminal of the CNOR. So vast was this plan that the government asked a British consultant to study the whole problem before agreeing to it. Mr (later Sir) Frederick Palmer commended the project but suggested that the CPR should join in also and so create another Union terminal. The CPR demurred and so CNR started work alone on the massive job of excavation that resulted in the 'big hole' in the centre of Montreal that was to stand for so many years unused due to the curtailment of all such projects during the thirties.

Final mention must be made of one of the most imaginative of all these railway consolidation projects. Reference to the map on page 116 will show the parallelism of the NTR and CNOR lines across the 'thousand mile gap' north of Lake Superior. CNR, when operating its major transcontinental trains, could route them through North Bay, up the Temiskaming and Northern Ontario Railway to Cochrane on the NTR, thence direct to Winnipeg. By the construction of what was known as the Long Lac Cut-Off, thirty miles in length, it was possible to have the best of both worlds, the use of the old CNOR line, then the cut-off, and then the NTR, with a saving of 102 miles over the previous CNOR route by way of Port Arthur.

Even without the advantage of the cut-off which was opened

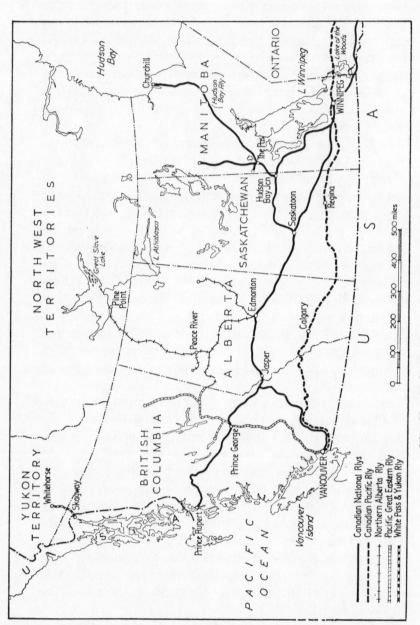

Map H: Main Lines in the West and North-West

in 1923, CNR had made great improvements to its long-distance passenger services. New trains between Montreal and Chicago, through Toronto, were inaugurated in 1926, a fast late-afternoon departure from Montreal giving a convenient late evening arrival at Toronto for the Inter-City Limited, followed by a night run to Chicago reached early the following day. In 1927, a second cross-Canada train was inaugurated and to mark the sixtieth anniversary of the founding of the Dominion, it was given the name 'The Confederation'. A third Montreal to Chicago service, as a day train from Montreal, was instituted. A second express, additional to the Ocean Limited and named the 'Acadian', started on the Montreal to Halifax run. All these, and many other new services, required much new rolling stock and this was provided in good measure. In the boom years of the late twenties, the government imposed no serious limitations upon such expenditure, with the result that CNR was soon equipped, at least for its mainline trains, as well as any railroad in North America. It even pioneered with radio receiving sets for passengers in parlour cars, the elegance of which made the headlines. Freight business was not neglected; in the year 1924 alone, 1,000 new box cars were placed in service.

Motive power had equal claim to attention since the locomotives taken over from the amalgamated lines were far from suitable for the new and heavier rolling stock and improved operating schedules. For freight work, powerful Mikado (2—8—2) and Santa Fe (2—10—2) types were designed; for passenger service, the first mountain-type (4—8—2) was also introduced. Even more far-seeing was the production in September 1925 of a self-contained diesel-electric passenger car, designed for light local service. Built at the Pointe St Charles shops of Canadian National, one of these units intended for service on the British Columbia coast was run from Montreal to Vancouver without its engines ever being shut off, making the trip in seventy-two hours, including five hours spent in station stops. These self-propelled cars were probably ahead of their day but they pointed ahead in a most surprising way.

The genius of Sir Henry Thornton can be seen behind many of these significant developments, even though so briefly summarised. So, also, can the chagrin of the CPR management as it had to face a steadily increasing tempo of competition and, worst of all, invasion by the CNR of what it regarded as its own territory in some parts of the west. Canadians grew accustomed to hearing of the travels and speeches of the two presidents, always couched in polite terms but sounding the note of alarm, in the case of the CPR with ever-mounting emphasis. So fierce was the competition, in all phases of operation, that probably some halt would have had to be called to it had not the world-wide economic depression of late 1929 caused this automatically. The fact, however, that such a competitive situation had developed within only six years of the official start of CNR is the best of all tributes to the work done by Sir Henry Thornton, certainly at great cost but with abiding benefit to the country as the years of the second world war would show. He had to wean public opinion away from the ideas that the years of poor service prior to 1918 had created, ideas about public operation of railways and (in some quarters) the poor operation of the GTR. In a land devoted to the free-enterprise system, he had to show that public ownership could give good management even though he could do nothing about the crushing financial burden that CNR continued to impose upon the national economy. He had to build up the morale of what had been a disorganised, discouraged and fragmented staff; this he did in good measure. He had to build up a permanent staff organisation—in operation, maintenance, design and finance—that would well serve the multi-million dollar corporation; this, too, he did well.

Inevitably he made enemies, some in the political field despite all that had been said about the non-political nature of CNR operation. In 1924, the Canadian House of Commons had established a select standing committee on railways and shipping. It provided a necessary public bridge between the public and railway administration, Sir Henry Thornton's annual appearances before the committee being important features of the Parliamentary year. The character of the committee changed after the start on 7 August 1930 of a new Conservative government under Mr R. B. (later Lord) Bennett, after a bitterly-fought election. The critical financial troubles of the times must have been, at least in part, responsible for the unusual political acrimony that marked the sittings of this committee of the new government. The records of the proceedings of the committee at its meetings in 1931 and 1932 do not make happy reading, but go some way to explain why, on 31 July 1932, Sir Henry Thornton left his posts with the railway to which he had contributed so much. The full circumstances of his departure still remain a mystery but there was no mystery at all about the widespread regret, especially among employees of all ranks in Canadian National Railways, when the news of his departure became public knowledge. He continued to live in Montreal but he died, after no more than a few months respite from the cares of office, on 14 March 1933. Canadian National Railways of today constitute his best memorial.

CHAPTER 11

Canadian Pacific Railway: 1886-1936

Through all the viscissitudes of these three turbulent decades of Canadian railroad development, the CPR continued its steady progress as the pioneer trans-Canada railway to the position of great distinction it had gained by the early years of the twentieth century as one of the world's greatest railways. In 1886 its total mileage, of lines built and acquired, was 4,406. Forty-five years later, it was operating a total mileage of well over 22,000 miles of both its own track and those of leased railways. Thereafter its total trackage decreased slightly but it remains today a truly remarkable railroad. It was fortunate in a continuity of outstanding leadership. William Cornelius Van Horne laid the foundations well and truly for its future greatness. He served as president from 1888 until he passed over this office in 1899 to his protegee, Thomas Shaughnessy, but he remained as chairman of the board until 1911 when he finally resigned; he died in Montreal on 11 September 1915, having been created a KCMG by Queen Victoria in 1894. Even today, the name—William Cornelius—is fraught with meaning amongst Canadian railway enthusiasts; he would not perhaps have approved of recent CPR actions some of which are related near the end of this volume.

Thomas Shaughnessy was a different but equally outstanding leader; it was said that Van Horne was the poker player, Shaughnessy a devotee of solitaire—a percipient distinction. He assumed the office of chairman of the board as well as continuing in the presidency when Van Horne resigned and

Page 143. (Above) CNR *passenger train from Chicago to Toronto emerging from the tunnel beneath the St Clair River at Sarnia, Ont., hauled by electric locos specially built for this underwater crossing;* (below) *a Canadian Pacific diesel locomotive at Windsor St Station, Montreal, after encountering a blizzard*

Page 144. *The main hall of Toronto Union Station*

so served until 1918. He then gave up the presidency but continued as chairman of the board until his death, also in Montreal, in 1923. Knighted in 1901, he was raised to the peerage in 1916 as Baron Shaughnessy. He had been succeeded as president by the vice-president and general counsel to the company, Edward Beatty, a distinguished lawyer. He was elected chairman of the board in 1924 and continued to hold both offices until 1942, being knighted in 1935. It may be helpful to note that Canadians have not been recipients of Royal honours since the twenties, apart from one short period in the mid-thirties, the Order of Canada being established in 1967 to provide recognition for such distinguished national service as earned the CPR pioneers their titles. Of the other great early figures, Donald Smith did not hold office in the company but he did serve as a director; he, too, was raised to the peerage as Lord Strathcona.

Sound management was reflected in the financial success of the company. Dividends on the common stock were paid without a break from 1885 to 1932, when for the next 12 years no payments were made. A few lean years at the start saw low returns but by 1905 a return of 6 per cent was paid. Good profits were made for the next twenty-five years, only the bad times of the thirties interfering with this solid financial achievement. Sales of the land so generously granted when the transcontinental line was built naturally helped, a large area being sold in 1914, for example, at a price of $17.80 per acre. Throughout its history the company has aimed at keeping its financial resources flexible. Fixed charges have therefore been kept to a minimum, the main capital being in the form of common stock. The contrast with the practice of the companies that were amalgamated to form CNR is interesting, but attention must be diverted from matters of high finance to the steady development of the physical property of the company.

As early as 1886 a modest start was made at building the first section of a good terminal at Montreal, combining from the outset offices of the company with the terminal facility. The first section of the famous Windsor Street Station, still the headquarters of the company, was opened for use in 1889. Repeated enlargements were made until the great building of today was completed in 1922 at a total cost of about $3.5 million. Another smaller terminal in the east end of the city was inherited with acquired lines; it was rebuilt as the Place Viger Station and Hotel in 1898. A loop line around the north end of the city was constructed before the turn of the century, providing access from both terminals to the main line to Quebec City and branch lines north of Montreal and facilitating freight movements from all parts of the extensive docks of the port of Montreal. A crossing of the St Lawrence to the south shore was another early essential since the Victoria Bridge was GTR property. A first bridge across the great river at Lachine was therefore built in 1886–87, being rebuilt and double-tracked with a much larger and stronger structure (in use today) in 1913. Another major facility in Montreal that had high priority once the railway was well established was a complete shop facility for the manufacture and maintenance of rolling stock. The Hochelaga shops were first built but were replaced by the Angus shops, in the east end of Montreal and conveniently located in relation to the loop line, which were finished in 1903 and were to produce much of the fine rolling stock that so distinguished the CPR.

Once the main line was well established, no time was lost in developing a network of lines in Ontario and Quebec, generally by acquisition of existing lines, and greatly to the chagrin of the GTR. Joseph Hickson had succeeded C. J. Brydges as general manager (the typically English title was retained) and he made loud and bitter complaints about the competition to which his lines would now be exposed. Complaints of this kind were to be heard many times in the next two decades, the CPR being as vociferous as any of the complainants in due course, and this despite the part that competition is supposed to play in the full exercise of free enterprise. Access to the junction point of Smith's Falls, in eastern Ontario, was acquired by 1887, and was to assume great importance as a CPR centre as its Ontario lines developed. A new railway to Peterborough and so to Toronto was the next development, and then to the extremity of south-western Ontario, Windsor being reached by 1890, in the heart of the GTR country. Here connection was made with the Michigan Central Railway (MCR) which was already using the southern part of this section of Ontario for a 'short-cut' across from Niagara Falls to Windsor; use was thus obtained of the tunnel under the Detroit River. A connection to Chicago followed, in competition with the GTR route through Sarnia. A strange footnote to this major CPR extension is that it was brought to public notice in 1971 that the CPR company did not own all the outstanding shares of the Ontario & Quebec Railway Co through which this main Montreal-Toronto-Windsor line was acquired! Of the 20,000 ordinary 6 per cent shares, 11,500 are believed to be held by the company with 8,500 still in the hands of 108 individual investors, almost one hundred years later.

In eastern Canada, the acquisition of the 'short line' to New Brunswick (p 94) gave access to Saint John. The subsequent leasing of the Carleton, City of Saint John Branch Railroad gave the CPR the great advantage of developing property in West Saint John, on the most convenient side of the harbour for port development. This was the beginning of the excellent port facilities, served by the CPR, that now feature West Saint John and make it such a worthy rival of the other major east coast port of Halifax with its strong CNR connections. A bridge was necessary over the famous Reversing Falls of the St John River in order to reach the central part of the city. The first structure was erected in 1885, to be replaced in 1913 by the great steel arched bridge that is still in use today spanning this unique natural feature, another of the major bridges that so distinguish the railways of Canada. CPR service in Nova Scotia had to wait, however, until 1912 when it was finally achieved through the leasing, as from the first day of January of that year for the usual period of 999 years, of the Dominion Atlantic Railway (DAR). This was the combination, again as usual, of several smaller lines, the first of which (from Windsor Junction to Annapolis) had been opened in 1869 and ran

Fig 2:   Crest on locomotive tenders of the Dominion Atlantic Railway (DAR)

down the south side of the famed Bay of Fundy, with its
world-record tides of up to 50 ft. Construction of this 200-mile
line necessitated the construction of a number of major bridges,
that at Windsor over the small Avon River requiring nine
spans for its length of 1,130 ft and piers adequate for the local
40-ft tides. Connection with the CPR lines was by means of a
ferry service across the fifty-mile width of the Bay from Saint
John to the small town of Digby, a passenger service only,
provided by a succession of fine 'cross-channel vessels' as they
may well be described. By securing running powers from

Windsor Junction over what is now the CNR, trains of the DAR gained access to the main Halifax terminal and so the CPR at last stretched from Atlantic to Pacific.

These eastern Canadian lines were all in settled country and so very different from the western main line, at least in its early days; it has been recorded that even in 1887 one of the small trains on the new railway over the prairies was beseiged by a pack of ravenous wolves. Despite all difficulties, operation continued without break. Connections with the United States had been made up the valley of the Red River from Winnipeg and by a link with the Northern Pacific Railway south of Vancouver that enabled CPR service to reach Seattle. Anxious to protect its specially favoured position in western Canada, the CPR management were fearful of the GTR acquiring connections with US lines and so 'invading their territory'. Accordingly they bought control of two US lines that ran from Sault Ste Marie, Michigan, thus permitting an easy connection by means of a bridge over the St Mary's River and ship locks. The Minneapolis, St Paul & Sault Ste Marie Railway (the Soo Line, as it came to be known) gave connections with St Paul, Minnesota, and thence north-west to cross into Canada to a connection with the main line at Moose Jaw, Saskatchewan. The Duluth, South Shore & Atlantic Railway gave a correspondingly alternative route to Winnipeg over US territory by way of Duluth. The GTR were therefore blocked from any possibility of expanding in this direction, only reaching the west through the ill-fated GTPR. One of the many 'ifs' of Canadian railway history is to consider what might have been the result if the GTR had first obtained these US links at Sault Ste Marie; Charles Hays might not have had his grandiose ideas that led to the GTPR; so the possibilities continue.

The privileged position of the Canadian Pacific in the west was naturally the subject of much public criticism from the outset. The new province of Manitoba did not like it and proceeded to grant charters to provincial railways despite the assurances the CPR had been given of restriction of competition for twenty years. One of the tall tales of these early days, but one that is quite true, concerns the 'Battle of Fort Whyte' some seven miles west of Winnipeg. Here the Red River Valley Railway, a provincially-authorised body, had to cross the CPR line on the level; a diamond crossing was installed by Red Valley men but taken out by company men and hauled off in triumph to the CPR yards. A locomotive had previously been derailed deliberately by the CPR on the route of the proposed invading railbed. Bloodshed was avoided but the emotions generated during the battle of nerves that lasted two weeks before the CPR's withdrawal must have been interesting to observe. More serious were complaints about the high freight rates being charged by the CPR, in the absence of competition or regulation, comparison with GTR rates in Ontario giving weight to the arguments from the west. The government saw that the situation could not continue and therefore passed an Act in 1888 repealing the monopoly clause, the policy of disallowance of provincial charters by the Federal Government was implicitly abandoned, and the company got a guarantee of the interest on a new loan of fifteen million dollars. Freight rates remained high; they were investigated by a number of commissions but this proved to be but the start of a dialogue about the iniquity of high rates on railway freight in Canada that continues to this day.

Despite the high freight rates, the west prospered; Canadian wheat became a world commodity and so its transport to ocean ports started to assume major proportions in the overall transport picture. Shipping facilities were developed on the Great Lakes and transhipment facilities at Montreal and other ocean ports, to the final sabotage of all the hopes entertained for grain shipment directly to the coast by rail over the NTR. Indicative of the importance of this traffic was the doubling of the main CPR line between Winnipeg and Fort William, at the head of Lake Superior, in 1906-09.

Far more important, however, from the operating point of view, were improvements to the main line in the mountains. The descent to Field after the Kicking Horse Pass through the

Rockies had been breasted was down seven miles at a gradient
of 4.5 per cent. Dangerous in descent, the 'Big Hill' was a
major operating problem for the east-bound trains that had
to climb it, trains having to be split and taken up in sections
by the small locomotives of the day working to the limit of
their capacity. This situation had to be improved. Construction
of the two spiral tunnels, now world famous, was completed
in 1909. The first, under Cathedral Mountain, is 3,206 ft long
and turns through 234 degrees in its descent of 48 ft between
portals. The second tunnel correspondingly drops 45 ft in its
length of 2,890 ft and turns through 232 degrees, the train
travelling in the opposite direction to its main journey in the
short level stretch between the adjacent portals of the two
tunnels. No matter how often one has the privilege of travelling
over this route, it retains its fascination as one imagines the
end of one's own train travelling in the opposite direction to
its head; to make the journey through the tunnels on the
footplate, as the writer has been privileged to do, is to enjoy
an unforgettable experience.

Use of the spiral tunnels immediately reduced the ruling
grade up the 'Big Hill' to 2.2 per cent compensated, still a
heavy climb but a great improvement over the original route.
(Picture, p 90.) Seven years later another equally important
improvement was put into use when the Connaught Tunnel
was completed. Sixty miles west of the important divisional
point of Field, the line turns south and starts another great
climb up the west side of the valley of the Beaver River in
order (originally) to reach Roger's Pass, climbing 1,900 ft in
17.1 miles with gradients of 2.2 per cent most of the way. The
route through the pass had many curves, and from the start
of operation it was plagued during winters by hazardous
avalanches. It can now be seen that, to a large extent, these
were the result of the burning, during construction operations,
of the trees on the slopes of the narrow valley that constitutes
the pass. Some serious accidents (one bad one in 1910) made
remedial measures imperative, and so the decision was made
to tunnel under the pass. The Connaught Tunnel, constructed

to take double track, is just over five miles long. Trains still have the long climb up from Beavermouth to the eastern portal of the tunnel but the summit elevation is 552 ft lower than the summit of the pass; four and a third miles are saved in distance travelled, and no less than the equivalent of seven complete circles of curvature were eliminated. A large ventilation installation was provided at the western (higher) portal; this is still in essential use even with diesel locomotives. Constant attention has been given to necessary minor improvements to the main Canadian Pacific line but it is today essentially the same as it was when the Connaught Tunnel improved it so much, apart only from the great change in signalling, now colour-light and centrally controlled throughout. The old route through Roger's Pass was utilised for the Trans-Canada Highway, completed in 1966, the railway benefitting from the extensive scientific study made of avalanches through and near the pass for three years before road construction started.

From the time of Van Horne, the Canadian Pacific Co provided more than just good railway service. Even before the Pacific coast had been reached, the idea was conceived of a steamship service from the new rail terminal to the Orient. This was established by Van Horne in 1891, after a mail subsidy had been assured and was the start of a notable ocean fleet. Lord Strathcona proved to be the greatest enthusiast for the 'All Red Route', a concept envisioning trans-Atlantic as well as trans-Pacific steamer services linked by the transcontinental trains of the CPR. Shaughnessy was a little more restrained but it was he who, early in 1903, arranged to purchase the entire Elder Dempster Atlantic fleet of fourteen vessels. The Allan Line (founded by Sir Hugh Allan, one of the early promoters of a railway across Canada) proved to be stiff competitors but the CPR won essential control of the line in 1909, although public transfer of control was not effected until 1915. The Cunard Line were well-established competitors and continued to be so until the virtual end of passenger steamship traffic on the North Atlantic. For fifty years, however, Canadian Pacific Ocean Services Limited provided one of the

excellent services, across both Atlantic and Pacific, that made
'travel by water' so pleasant a mode of transportation. The
'White Empresses' gradually developed a reputation all their
own and were well known around the world.

Inland and coastal steamship services were also a part of
the steadily expanding 'transportation empire' of the Canadian
Pacific, of which the Bay of Fundy Ferry Service was just a
small part. A fine fleet was built up on the Great Lakes,
including two excellent passenger vessels. These were built in
Scotland, sailed to Montreal, cut in two, towed up the St
Lawrence in two sections, and through its small canals in
days long before the St Lawrence Seaway, and then reconnected
in a Great Lakes shipyard. These ships provided an alternative
to rail travel for passengers who had time for the delightful
journey between Port McNicol on Georgian Bay and the
Lakehead. Similar but more limited services were provided
on some of the lakes in the mountain valleys of British Columbia,
giving connections with CPR rail services. (Picture, p 53.)
And on the Pacific coast another notable fleet of passenger
vessels was built up to provide connections between Vancouver
and points on Vancouver Island, Victoria notably, and also
up the coast to Alaska. All but the ferry services between
Vancouver and Nanaimo, and Saint John and Digby, have
now gone but in their day these fine services added their
quota to the proud claim that the CPR was the 'world's greatest
transportation system'.

So also did the hotels that were yet another of Van Horne's
inspirations. Before the end of the nineteenth century, plans
had been drawn up for the start of the Chateau Frontenac
on its commanding site adjacent to the Plains of Abraham in
Quebec City. It was the first of a chain of 'railway hotels'
across the country developed by the CPR, paralleled at a later
date by the corresponding chain of CNR hotels, in combination constituting one of the unique features of the Canadian
railway world. In Quebec City, Winnipeg, Regina, Calgary
and Vancouver notable CPR hotels provided all-year-round
service to the highest standards, the Chateau Frontenac in

Quebec City still being the 'favourite hotel' of many experienced travellers. Summer hotels were also built at attractive
resorts served by the CPR. Toronto and Montreal came relatively late into the CPR hotel picture but they, too, now have
fine railway-operated hostelries. In great contrast to the
Royal York (Toronto) and the Chateau Champlain (Montreal)
was the simple but popular wooden-building hotel on the
station platform at McAdam Junction, an important railway
meeting-place in earlier days in southern New Brunswick.
This was indeed a railway hotel, presided over by a wonderful
hostess whom the writer was privileged to know and whose
careful attention counterbalanced the sounds of locomotives
on the tracks around.

The CPR early gained a reputation for fine rolling stock,
to North American standards, and good and efficient locomotives. Special observation cars were built for use on the
all-sleeping-car Trans Canada Limited, the first of the major
named post-war trains introduced on 1 June 1919. Indicative
of early interest in locomotives was the introduction in 1918
of the practice of naming locomotives, a pleasant acknowledge-
ment of public interest, but one that unfortunately did not
persist for many years. In those days, CPR locomotives were
but little different from the general pattern followed on North
American lines, with 2—6—0s, 4—6—0s and 4—6—2s pre-
dominating, all with the usual display of accessories that is
in such contrast to standard British locomotive design. The
1200 class of 4—6—2s was especially notable since they were
powerful engines for their day but so carefully designed that
they could run on any line throughout the entire CPR system,
despite local loading limitations. Described as belonging to
'Class G—5—a', these sturdy locomotives were still in use as
the steam era came to an end, one of the class being the last
steam locomotive to be built by the CPR in its own Angus
shops in Montreal, outshopped in 1944.

It was in the great railroading days of the late twenties that
the CPR introduced locomotives of its own design which came
to be recognised far beyond the borders of Canada as

outstanding machines. For working the heavy grades over the Rockies between Calgary and Revelstoke, a class of 2—10—4s was designed, and gradually improved, that gave Canada a stud of one of the finest heavy-haulage locomotives in North America. No 5900 was the class leader, built by Montreal Locomotive Works (MLW) in 1929; eventually a group of thirty-six of these fine machines to a steadily improved design was at work, converted to oil-burning after early experience with coal. In 1940 the writer had the happy privilege of riding the footplate of one of these great machines from Banff, 'over the top' at Hector, and down through the Spiral Tunnels to Field. It was an experience never to be forgotten. The driver was one of the top-link men from Calgary. With one hand always on the regulator and the other controlling the cut-off, he showed clearly the skill of the true expert in bringing his train of twelve heavy coaches, without any assistance, up to the summit near Hector without ever a slip of the wheels, dropping only to a speed of 25 mph as the descent through the tunnels commenced.

In strange contrast was a similar experience twenty years later, again with a top-link driver, but this time in the cab of the leading unit of four diesel engines, with all its creature comforts. The driver turned his control lever full on after the start and then sat back throughout the big climb, his eyes ever watchful ahead but his hands free for other things, automatic controls demonstrating their wonder again even as they removed the artistry from the driving.

Two 4—8—4s (class K—1—a) were built in 1928 but, in strange contrast with CNR experience, they did not prove successful and no more were built, Nos 3100 and 3101 usually working the night 'sleeper' between Montreal and Toronto before finishing their days in the west. On the other hand, two very successful 2—8—4s were constructed for the subsidiary THBR, also by MLW, but in 1928, for hauling heavy freight trains from Hamilton to Niagara Falls, up a heavily graded line. Locomotive designs rarely cause widespread controversy but the last major design introduced by the CPR certainly did, two groups of semi-streamlined 4—4—4s intended for high-speed passenger service. Some had 80-in driving wheels and a boiler pressure of 300 psi. The five that were built in 1936 were seldom used to their full speed potential; their characteristic propensity for slipping prevented their use with heavy trains, but they remained in secondary service until 1958. Some thought them to be attractive-looking machines; others, the poorest-looking modern locomotives of the CPR, their unusual wheel arrangements and heavy trailing bogie giving them an almost unbalanced appearance.

In great contrast were the splendid Royal Hudsons. Introduced in 1929, they incorporated all the best features of North American locomotive design of the time and were really handsome machines, a real effort having been made to give them clean-cut lines. They had 22in diameter cylinders with a 30in stroke, a boiler pressure of 275 psi. and driving wheels 75in in diameter; nominal tractive effort was 42,250 lb. Finished in maroon livery and always maintained in immaculate condition, they came to be regarded as amongst the finest-looking machines on North American rails, and their performance was in keeping with their appearance. Eventually, the class numbered sixty-five, and No 2850 had the distinction of hauling the Royal Train in 1939 over the CPR part of its return cross-country route. Thereafter No 2850, and eventually Nos 2820 to 2864, carried large golden crowns mounted on the forward part of the running board skirt, the class being then called the Royal Hudsons. The splendid train, probably the last Royal Train to travel the width of the country, carried King George VI and his gracious Queen in the early summer of that fateful year across Canada from sea to sea. A carefully planned tour was provided to the west coast along a different route, the entire journey being a splendid example of co-operative effort on the part of CNR and CPR, co-operation quite different from that which the years of depression made mandatory and to which attention must now be directed.

CHAPTER 12

Years of Depression and War
1932-46

The financial crisis of October 1929 marked a turning point in the history of Canada, and equally so for the railways of Canada. From the unbridled optimism and booming economy of the later twenties, the whole country was plunged into an era of such widespread unemployment that public welfare had to be instituted on a scale that led directly into the welfare state of today. Traffic on the railways of Canada was cut in half between the boom year of 1928 and the depth of the depression in 1932–33. The number of passengers carried in the year 1932 was smaller than for any previous year since 1902. At that time, the railway mileage was only 44 per cent of what it was in 1932; the country's population was about one-half of what it was to become thirty years later. This economic disaster came immediately after the period of intense competition between CNR and CPR, competition openly promoted by Sir Henry Thornton and the CNR management as they made such valiant efforts to develop their strange organisation into a unified railway system, giving the public of Canada service as good as, if not better than, that of the CPR. The CPR had to respond, in kind, in order to maintain their own position, even though this meant a departure from their previously rather conservative progress, and even from their long-time prudent financial policies. Both railways made vast expenditures in the later twenties, financed generally through fixed securities for which the interest had always to be found. Common-stock holders of the CPR had their dividends cut and eventually eliminated. CNR management saw their net operating revenue fall from over $42 million in 1928 to a mere $2,313 in 1931.

The situation in which the railways found themselves was so serious that the president of the CPR publicly suggested to Sir Henry Thornton that he should propose the establishment of an independent tribunal to study the whole question of transportation in Canada with a view to suggesting some ameliorative measures. Sir Henry suggested such a step to the government on 25 June 1931, as a result of which a Royal Commission—yet another—was appointed in November of that year. (Canada must hold some sort of record for the number of Royal Commissions that have reported upon its railways and their problems). The Royal Commission of 1931 was unusual in that it was made up of seven commissioners, headed by Mr Justice Duff of the Supreme Court of Canada. Lord Ashfield, Chairman of the London Underground, was one member; so also was L. F. Loree, President of the Delaware and Hudson Co (of the USA). The other four members were eminent Canadians with no direct interest in or detailed knowledge of railroading. Hearings before the commission produced a great deal of interesting and useful factual information, even as they also revealed widespread differences of opinion all across the country as to the best solution to the obvious problem. There were those who urged amalgamation of the two major lines as the only solution. Equally vociferous were those to whom any idea of such a vast corporate enterprise, under either public or private ownership, was anathema. The commissioners saw the railways in action and had many discussions with practical operating staff members but, as can be seen today, they finally developed a decided bias against CNR.

They heard much about the extravagancies of Sir Henry Thornton, but seemed to disregard completely the almost incredible problem with which he was faced when he took office and the task he had in forging the divergent portions of what he inherited into a unified railway. They seemed to turn a blind eye to the multiplicity of lines for which the CPR were responsible. Some duplication of lines was inevitable, such as the two sets of double tracks approaching Montreal from the west since both railways have to cross over to the island of Montreal at the same point (Ste Anne de Bellevue); 'racing' along these tracks, especially with suburban trains, was not unknown; it had, indeed, been encouraged by Van Horne. But it would have been difficult to find a logical explanation for the extra line that the CPR built into Toronto, duplicating and running generally within sight of the main line of the CNR for a good hundred miles.

Some indication of the competitive spirit that had been generated was given even while the commission was sitting. Early in the thirties CNR announced that they were reducing the overall running time of the late afternoon trains between Montreal and Toronto (334 miles) to six hours flat, including six intermediate stops. They had a splendidly maintained double track with few grades of any consequence and only one bad curve (at Kingston) to limit speeds but, even so, the new schedule involved locomotive work of the highest order. Despite the fact that more than half of their route was single track, with no large centres to be served by intermediate stops, CPR felt bound to respond. They could not meet the six hour schedule but, surprisingly, they did evolve a schedule that gave an overall running time between Montreal and Toronto, despite that long single track, of six hours and fifteen minutes.

In order to achieve this remarkable schedule, the CPR had to make the best possible use of their double-tracked section, the 124 miles from Montreal West to Smith's Falls, two suburban stops outside Montreal being almost mandatory before the fast run could commence. They cut the running time for this stretch to 109 minutes westbound, representing an average speed of 68.2 mph. For a short period, these two trains were the fastest scheduled runs of the world. Reaction in the United Kingdom cut short this brief spell of glory. The Great Western Railway (of the UK) felt compelled to accelerate again their Cheltenham Flyer in order to regain the world-speed-title but the CPR runs continued for a few months. The writer had the privilege of travelling on one of the west-bound trains during this period of exciting running, and the log of the run is summarised in the accompanying table. Loads were naturally kept light but there were eight coaches on this particular day, well loaded, giving a total weight of at least 600 tons (so heavy is standard Canadian passenger stock). The class leader of the Royal Hudsons (No 2800) was at the head of the train, and the record shows what could be achieved over a clear track. Much of the run was at a speed over 75 mph, and 80 mph was exceeded briefly. For almost all of the rest of the run to Toronto single track had to be used; opposing trains were all safely tucked away in passing loops—at what cost to orderly scheduling can only be imagined—and the running, on a single track, was even more exciting than the straightforward run to Smith's Falls, although speeds were not quite so high.

It was wonderful; but it was folly. Clearly such unbridled competition could not continue. The leaders of the two great railways admitted this in their critical evidence to the Royal Commission. The CPR views were well known and were repeated by the president to the commissioners; 'Under existing conditions in Canada, the only solution which will stand the test of the country's necessities is a consolidation through a lease on a profit-sharing basis of the government railways and the Canadian Pacific'. The use of the term 'government railways' showed that Canadian National had still to win recognition in at least this quarter. The views of Sir Henry Thornton were not well known and so his evidence was awaited with special interest. 'Amalgamation', he said, 'would be definitely repugnant to the people of the Dominion . . . (and urged) the development of an intensive degree of co-operation between the two companies in order that waste in whatever form it is found may be eliminated'. He also gave an outline of an administrative arrangement that would 'necessarily involve the reduction of political interference to a minimum'. It was

TABLE 1: Canadian Pacific Railway

CPR late afternoon train Montreal to Toronto.
Mid-summer, 1931
Fine weather.
Locomotive No 2800, CPR 4—6—4 o.c.
Load: eight cars, including one dining-car;
gross tonnage 600.

Station	Booked Time ms	Miles	Running Time ms
Montreal West	0.00	0.0	0.00
Dorval	5.00	4.9	6.30
Lakeside	—	7.9	9.05
Beaurepaire	—	12.2	12.30
Ste. Anne's	14.00	15.7	15.20
Vaudreuil	17.00	19.0*	18.20
St. Lazare	21.00	23.7	22.30
St. Clet	26.00	29.7	27.45
De Beaujeu	31.00	35.5	32.40
Dalhousie Mills	37.00	41.7*	38.05
Green Valley	43.00	49.3	44.35
Apple Hill	50.00	58.0	51.35
Monklands	55.00	63.4	56.15
Avonmore	59.00	68.2*	60.05
Finch	65.00	74.3	64.35
Chesterville	71.00	82.00*	70.30
Winchester	76.00	87.9	75.10
Inkerman	—	91.1	77.45
Mountain	82.00	95.9	81.30
Bedell	89.00	103.2	87.45
Swan	—	106.9*	91.00
Burritts	—	111.1	94.25
Merrickville	99.00	114.9	97.30
Rosedale	—	119.9	101.30
Smiths Falls	109.00	124.0	105.50

* indicates service slacks to 60 mph

Average speeds: Montreal West to Smiths Falls: 70.6 mph
Mileage 67–77; 78.3 mph
Mileage 77–87; 79.1 mph
Mileage 87–97; 75.0 mph

not without significance that a newly elected Conservative government was now in office in Ottawa. The commission was not persuaded by the arguments for amalgamation and so favoured continued moderate competition, co-operation where possible, replacement of the CNR board of directors by three trustees, and emancipation of the 'National Railways' (still not Canadian National) from 'political interference and community pressure'. A Bill to implement the finding of the commission was introduced into the Senate of Canada in October 1932, receiving Royal assent only in May 1933 after long and fervent debate.

In December 1933, three trustees were appointed to replace the CNR board, under the chairmanship of C. P. Fullerton. They appointed S. J. Hungerford (previously acting president) as president in place of Sir Henry, but their trusteeship was short lived. When, in August 1935, a Liberal government was returned to office in the general election, one of its early acts (in 1936) was to abolish the trustees, replacing them with the more usual board of (seven) directors, clearly responsible to the government of the country. Beyond this, the results of all the work of the Royal Commission—apart from assembling a great deal of useful information—were almost negligible with the exception of one small piece of co-operation. No arbitration tribunal, as suggested by the commission, was ever established. Previous competition continued, although not to the extreme degree that had immediately preceded the establishment of the commission. The only concrete result was the establishment of a joint executive committee of the two railways which, in turn, appointed a joint technical committee. After investigation of what could be done in eliminating duplicate services, the two railways did agree to 'pool' their passenger services between Montreal and Toronto, and between Ottawa and Toronto, but that was essentially all. Gradually the two great systems learned to 'live together'. Slowly and gradually the national economy improved. Wheat shipments, a mainstay of railroad income, slowly increased and so did railroad earnings. Dividends on the widely held common stock of the CPR were resumed in 1944. Both passenger and freight movements continued to improve in the years immediately prior to the outbreak of war in 1939, and by 1940 freight had reached a level comparable with the situation in about 1920.

The rather strange pooling arrangement, which must often have puzzled visitors to Canada between 1933 and 1965, when it was abolished, led to some interesting operating procedures. Both railways continued to operate their overnight sleeping-car trains between Montreal and Toronto, but here easy schedules were possible in order to give convenient arrival times. The corresponding night trains between Ottawa and Toronto used CPR and CNR equipment, and ran on CPR tracks between Ottawa and Smith's Falls where through cars were attached or detached to and from the CPR night sleeper between Montreal and Toronto. There was a degree of co-operation with the slower day trains but the main evidence of the 'pooling' was in the fast late-afternoon trains between the two big cities. These used the CPR Windsor Street Station in Montreal for arrival and departure, but naturally used the fine double track of the CNR for the main journey. To effect this, a short cross-over junction was installed at Dorval, eleven miles outside Montreal, where the CNR and CPR tracks converged for their parallel run to Ste Anne de Bellevue. Passenger stock was predominantly CNR, including some of the finest dining cars ever to run in Canada; good schedules were maintained, never far from the dramatic six hours of the early thirties despite the extra CPR suburban stops in Montreal. Running was exemplary, this being the crack International Limited of Canadian National. But staunch and loyal CPR employees never really did get used to the idea of a CNR train using the facilities of Windsor Street Station, Montreal; CNR employees had similar reactions.

So important has been this Montreal to Toronto service from the earliest days of Canadian railway history, that a typical run may be of interest. An outline only can be given, and only for that part of the run from Toronto to Brockville (still 126 miles from Montreal), since at this point through cars from Ottawa were detached and it was in these that the writer made many memorable journeys in post-war years. The standard make-up of the train from Toronto to Brockville was fifteen cars, including two dining cars, giving a loaded weight of 1,100 tons. For working this and comparable trains, CNR were fortunate in having a large stud of 4—8—4s, the later members of which were certainly among the finest steam locomotives to run on North American lines. With their large tenders, it was possible for them to work the 330-mile Toronto–Montreal run with stops for coal only at the efficient coal stages at Belleville and Brockville, 113 and 208 miles from Toronto, respectively, taking water at five stops, with a final run of 127 miles into Montreal.

Additional stops were made at Oshawa, Port Hope and Kingston prior to Brockville, and at Cornwall, Montreal West and Westmount thereafter, mileages being as shown on the accompanying table, which gives a summary log of a run from Toronto to Brockville on a wild winter night in the mid-fifties. There is a $4\frac{1}{2}$ mile climb out of Toronto, up to Scarborough Junction, most of it at about 1 in 100, a gradual descent into Oshawa and thereafter generally level track with the bad approach curve to Kingston Station already mentioned. With this background information, the log can be left to speak for itself, averages of almost 70 mph with a more than thousand-ton train for such relatively short runs between stops providing clear evidence of what the railways of Canada could do in the greatest days of steam haulage.

In view of the way in which Canadian National Railways was formed, it is not surprising that it was not until the late twenties that the newly integrated staff could prepare loco-motive designs to serve the widely varying needs of the new system. It is, indeed, remarkable that as early as June 1927 the first of the 4—8—4s that were to make CNR locomotive practice so well and favourably known was out-shopped from the works of MLW, following an initial 6000 class. This was No 6100. In October 1927, it was exhibited at the centenary celebrations of the Baltimore & Ohio Railroad, in the good but quite fitting company of *King George V* of the Great Western Railway of England. It proved to be the first of 203 locomotives of this type that were built to gradually improved design before the diesels took over. More than 150 of the group of Northerns, as they were known, had two cylinders $25\frac{1}{2}$ in in diameter with a 30 in stroke; 73 in diameter drivers; and a boiler pressure of 250 psi. Their class designa-

TABLE 2: Canadian National Railways

CNR-CPR late afternoon Pool train; Toronto to Montreal.
Mid-winter 1955.
Strong side wind with heavy rain.
Locomotive No 6210, CNR 4—8—4 o.c.
Load: fifteen cars, including two dining cars, well filled;
gross tonnage 1,100.

Station	Booked Time ms	Miles	Running Time ms	mph
Toronto	0.00	0.0	0.00	—
Danforth	—	5.2	11.35	27.0
Scarboro Jnc.	18.00	8.8	17.45	35.0
Port Union	—	16.2	24.45	63.4
Pickering	30.00	22.3	29.35	75.8
Whitby	36.00	28.9	34.50	75.6
Oshawa	—	33.3	39.40	54.8
	43.00⎱ 0.00⎰	—	0.00	—
Bowmanville	—	9.7	10.15	56.6
Port Hope	—	29.7	26.35	73.6
	30.00⎱ 0.00⎰	—	0.00	—
Cobourg	8.00	6.7	9.00	44.5
Colborne	19.00	21.3	21.00	73.0
Brighton	25.00	28.9	26.55	77.2
Smithfield	—	32.4	29.40	76.5
Trenton Jnc.	33.00	38.0	34.05	76.2
Belleville	45.00	50.1	44.35	69.00
			0.00	—
(Coal Stage)	—	1.2	5.30	—
	0.00	—	0.00	—
Shannonville	13.00	6.00	9.15	38.8
Marysville	19.00	12.5	16.55	50.9
Napanee	28.00	20.6	24.15	66.5
Fredericksburg	32.00	25.7	28.55	65.8
Ernestown	38.00	31.5	33.35	74.7
Collin's Bay	45.00	39.1	40.55	62.3
Kingston	—	46.5	49.25	52.3
	58.00⎱ 0.00⎰	0.0	0.00	—
Rideau	5.00	4.7	7.00	40.3
Findley	15.00	12.9	16.00	54.6
Gananoque Jnc.	20.00	19.1	21.20	69.9
Lansdowne	—	26.5	27.35	71.0
Mallorytown	33.00	34.7	36.55	52.7
(Coal Stage)	—	46.8	48.10	64.5
			49.50	
Brockville	51.00	47.4	51.20	—

Average Toronto to Oshawa   50.4 mph   Belleville to Kingston   56.5 mph
Speeds: Oshawa to Port Hope   67.4 ,,   Kingston to Brockville 58.0 ,,
      Port Hope to Belleville 67.4 ,,   (Coal stage)

tions, from 'U—2—a' to 'U—2—h', are not meaningful to those not in close touch with locomotive design, even though they do indicate the gradual development of the design. Equipped throughout with roller-bearings, later models had also a booster auxiliary with a tractive effort of 12,000 lb, to assist the 57,000 lb tractive potential of the main engine as necessary, the adhesion factor being 4.33. The engines themselves weighed 180 tons, the Vanderbilt tenders no less than 124 tons when loaded with 18 tons of coal and 11,600 gallons of water. They were stoker-fired, and some were equipped with Walschaert's valve-gear.

These details are given for the CNR Northern design since it probably did represent, in its final form, the peak of Canadian locomotive practice, and this with no disrespect to the splendid Royal Hudsons and the great Selkirk class of the CPR. The class as a whole were not particularly 'beautiful' locomotives, not nearly so attractive in appearance as the Royal Hudsons, although their massive character clearly indicated their haulage potential. They followed a small group of 4—6—4s of comparable design that were, however, really delightful-looking engines. This was the small 5700 group, similar in essentials to the Northerns but with 80-in driving wheels. Finished in green livery (the Northerns were generally all black with good lining and finish) and equipped with large Vanderbilt tenders, they served well on the fast Toronto-Montreal service until train loads became too heavy for them, their duties then being assumed by the Northerns. In the same tradition of appearance were the ten 6400s (4—8—4s) which represented the ultimate development of the Northern design. With streamlined bodies, designed after careful wind-tunnel tests conducted in the Ottawa laboratories of the National Research Council, and so displaying few of the usual North American accessories draped around the boilers, finished in green with careful lining, they were truly magnificent machines. No 6400 provided the CNR haulage for the Royal Train in 1939 and was later exhibited at the World's Fair of that year in New York. They cost $150,000 each, a figure that is mentioned if only to indicate the large capital investment in steam locomotives that was so soon to disappear.

As an indication of some of the operating problems faced by the motive-power departments of both major Canadian railways, there may be mentioned a small class of CNR Mikados (2—8—2s) built in 1936 with boilers specially designed for use in areas where available water was unduly hard. Nos 3800 to 3805 spent their working lives between Watrous and Melville, in Saskatchewan, for this unusual reason. They were built by the Canadian Locomotive Co (CLC) in Kingston. Although in the early years locomotives for Canadian railways were generally imported from Great Britain and the United States, once the building of locomotives in Canada started, in 1853, Canadian railways gradually came to be equipped with engines made in Canada. In more recent years, the two great company shops—Pointe St Charles for CNR and Angus for CPR, both in Montreal—have turned out many notable machines but their production has always had to be supplemented by the products of private manufacturers. In these recent years this has meant essentially from either MLW or CLC in Kingston. Both these great plants developed enviable reputations as locomot.ve builders and built up appreciable export business. With the change to diesels, the Kingston plant has disappeared, but MLW has become one of North America's most notable producers of diesel locomotives, especially following the termination of this activity on the part of the American Locomotive Company with which MLW had close links.

Visitors to Montreal or Ottawa can still see in the museums mentioned in Chapter 15 fine examples of the steam loco-motives that served Canada so well. The Ottawa museum now contains part of the CNR Museum Train that toured the country from 1953 to 1957. (Picture, p 72.) Although actually hauled by a modern 2—6—0, the little train of ancient yellow-painted coaches had at its head two veterans. CNR No 247 was one of the very few true saddle-tank engines ever to run on Canadian lines; built in 1894 for the GTR, it is a 0—6—0 saddle-tank of somewhat strange appearance with its North American appendages as well as its tank. No 40 is a 4—4—0 built in 1872 at the Portland Works as a woodburner, serving the Chaudiére Valley Railway where she was located by members of the CRHA and repatriated by CNR in an exchange. Now well preserved in the National Museum of Science and Technology, with their train, they are in strange contrast to the diesel engines now universal on Canadian lines following the great conversion.

The change to diesel haulage was a post-war development, the pioneering efforts of CNR under Sir Henry Thornton having had little immediate effect on motive power practice in Canada. The years of war were to demonstrate vividly what the railways meant to Canada but even before the years of this phenomenal performance there were a few signs of the profound changes that post-war years were to bring. Road traffic was beginning to increase appreciably; the first modern inter-city highways were being built. A first casualty from the inroads of road traffic were the electric railways of Canada. Started well before the turn of the century, generally serving well populated urban areas and the surrounding territories, the 'inter-urbans' (as they were sometimes called) played a very important part in the Canadian transportation picture in the early years of the twentieth century, reaching a surprising total mileage of 1,737 in 1925. There were some small lines in the Maritime Provinces. Around Quebec City, the Quebec Railway Light & Power Co operated a service that ran as far as the famous shrine at Ste Anne de Beaupré, this being a most scenic line along the north shore of the St Lawrence, passing the beautiful Montmorency Falls. The Montreal & Southern Counties Railway (eventually purchased by CNR) crossed the Victoria Bridge from a downtown terminal in Montreal and gave good service to suburbs on the south shore, its main line extending as far as Granby, fifty-three miles away. Even the smaller city of Ottawa had its convenient electrical railway system with an extension beyond the city four miles to the west in its own private right-of-way, a familiar pattern around Canadian cities.

In Ontario, the Hydro Electric Power Commission, formed in 1906 as one of the great pioneer publicly-owned utilities, actively promoted the development of electric inter-urban railways and in the twenties itself operated systems in and around Toronto, Windsor, Guelph and Peterborough. These were later disposed of, that in Toronto to the Toronto Transportation Commission. Around Windsor, the electric railway provided a convenient 'belt line service' linking up several mainline steam-operated railways and providing yard service. In the far west, the British Columbia Light & Power Co operated an extensive system around Vancouver with a total mileage, at one time, of 375 miles serving much of the 'lower mainland', the great plain at the mouth of the Fraser River. There was even a small electric line connecting two northern mining towns in Ontario, Cobalt via Haileybury to New Liskeard, 200 miles north of the nearest similar system.

The Niagara, St Catharines & Toronto Railway (NStCTR) was one of the busiest of these electrical railways, serving the well populated area around St Catharines and Niagara Falls, the availability of cheap power from which probably led to the opening of an electrically-operated line from St Catharines to Thorold as early as 1887. Its main line extended through several of these small towns (as they then were) for a total distance of seventy-five miles. In 1921 the system carried well over eight million passengers. For a short period it could call itself an 'international railway' since running powers were obtained across the old 'Honeymoon' bridge into Niagara Falls, New York. Here connections were made with the high-speed electric service to Buffalo, and thence to other cities in northern New York State. It was a pleasant experience to cross by boat from Toronto to Port Dalhousie and there to board one of the fine multi-car trains of the NStCTR for the exciting ride up the Niagara escarpment and on to Niagara Falls itself. But all this was quickly to disappear as the automobile started its relentless climb in public favour and use. All mainline service ceased in 1947. A very limited service between Thorold and Port Colbourne did continue until

March 1959 so that the Niagara line can lay claim to having been probably the first and the last of Canada's inter-urban electric railways. The freight service provided, on a small scale, by the Cornwall Street Railway, Light & Power Co in this eastern Ontario city did not stop until 9 October 1971 but its passenger service was then long in the past.

These electric railway operations in post-war years, with the notable exception of services in Toronto as will later be seen, were anachronisms in a way; each continued for some special local reason. The automobile, and more particularly petrol- and then diesel-engined bus services, provided competition they could not meet. Even the stringent limitations upon motor fuel during later war years did not prevent this new form of transportation from displacing almost all Canadian electrical rail services by the 1940s.

In all other respects, however, the railways of Canada were strained to the limit of their resources by the demands of war. In 1944, an all-time record of over sixty million passengers were carried. Of the eighty-eight billion ton-miles of freight moved in 1945, over 70 per cent was carried by the railways of Canada, 25 per cent by water and only just over 3 per cent by road. When it is recalled that, in addition to providing Canadian contingents of all fighting services, the Dominion was the fourth largest supplier of war material, its production only exceeded by that of Great Britain, the United States and the Soviet Union, with most of it being shipped through 'eastern Canadian ports' (as they had to be known in wartime), the wartime record of the railways of Canada is indeed a staggering one. There were no new major facilities, no major new lines but rather the closest co-operation of all rail carriers, under ultimate government control, with superb maintenance despite all difficulties and operating achievements the record of which could well fill a companion volume to this.

Although Montreal and other St Lawrence ports continued to operate except for the few winter months when ice conditions closed them, the activities of German submarines in the Gulf of St Lawrence were so serious at one time that great reliance had to be placed on the facilities of the 'eastern Canadian ports'. These were, naturally, Saint John and Halifax. Both played their part fully in this wartime epic of transportation, as did both CPR and CNR. Halifax, however, was in a special position with its direct access from the open Atlantic, its outer wharves capable of docking the largest ships in the world, and its magnificent inner harbour an ideal mooring ground for use in assembling convoys. It was, therefore, Canada's main port of shipment throughout the war both for the export of war supplies and the embarkation and disembarking of troops. It had, however, only one rail link with the rest of Canada, and so with the United States, consisting of 185 miles of single track (except for passing loops) from Catamount, twelve miles west of Moncton, to Windsor Junction, sixteen miles west of Halifax. This was indeed the lifeline of Canada. Its wartime traffic volume is thought to be unsurpassed in the entire world history of railroading.

The port of Halifax, and the CNR line that serves it, had been under similar pressure (although each was under different auspices at that time) during the first world war, and this experience was available to guide the authorities in 1940. One immediate result was the decision to install Centralised Traffic Control (CTC) from Moncton to Halifax in 1941. Had this not been done, it is difficult to imagine what the operating consequences might have been. Control offices were located in Moncton and Halifax, the system being divided into two parts at Truro. Indicative of the enhanced efficiency in operation is the fact that the overall speed of freight trains over the first section was increased from 13.84 to 18.06 mph. So closely were trains controlled that, with power-operated switches, it was not uncommon for passing trains to use one of the passing loops without either one having to stop. This first section (Moncton to Truro) is a difficult one to work even under normal conditions, running through hilly country with the result that the entire route can accurately be described as a switchback, with extensive curvature and almost continuous grades, as high as 1.47 per cent. The line has to carry, in addition to all Halifax traffic, that for Prince Edward Island (taking off at Sackville) and the heavy coal and steel traffic from Sydney (coming in at Truro). Feeding into Moncton, and available for westbound traffic, are three main lines—the old ICR to Levis and Montreal, the much-maligned NTR through Edmunston and Quebec to the west (for these few brief years, it finally came into its own), and the older line turning south to Saint John with connections to the United States through US lines in the State of Maine. All traffic on these three lines, however, from and to all over the continent, had to be carried by that single critical railway from Moncton to Halifax.

The CTC system was installed in five months and very quickly showed its effectiveness. As an example, not too long after its installation, there were at one time twenty-two trains 'on the board' between Moncton and Amherst (48.3 miles) with an average operating spacing of only 2.2 miles. On this first 'switchback' section to Truro, there were four regular passenger trains every day, each one consisting of from fourteen to sixteen cars, one passenger train to The Island, as well as fifteen through freights together with local freight service. On a typical day, train movements over the 125 miles would vary between fifty and eighty. All trains had to stop at Springhill Junction for coal and water, and this involved extra train movements.

Between Truro and Halifax, the grades and curvature were easier (maximum gradient 0.9 per cent) and so higher speeds were possible. Its daily load was normally about fifty train movements over the forty-five miles, since it had trains from Halifax to Cape Breton Island to compensate for those that left the main line at Sackville and Truro. It was not uncommon to have twenty trains 'on the board' at Halifax. This was reasonably heavy normal traffic for a single line, but to it had to be added all the special trains that were needed for wartime purposes. Extra freight trains could be scheduled to fit in with existing timetables but not so the fleet of special trains necessary when one of the big troop-carrying ocean vessels arrived or departed.

Both the famous 'Queens' of the Cunard Line became well known visitors to Halifax harbour, although never mentioned in the press at the time. They and similar vessels could carry up to as many as 14,000 troops. Their transport required no less than twenty-eight trains, complete with all services such as dining cars and baggage cars. Empty trains had to be brought into Halifax; fortunately, the yards were adequate for their storage even though at some distance from the main terminal. The trains had to be loaded and dispatched at intervals of between thirty and forty-five minutes, in addition to all other regular train services. And this was completed in less than twenty-four hours as a regular procedure. On one occasion, eighteen such special trains were handled, in addition to all regular traffic, in eleven and one-half hours. No more need be said since even cursory knowledge of railroad operations will leave no doubt in any reader's mind as to the superb organisation and operation of these astounding movements, all carried out with no fanfare, with relatively little delay to normal service, and with no accidents.

This was typical of Canadian railway war service. The Railway Association of Canada acted as one co-ordinating medium, and the government's transport controller used advisory joint committees whenever necessary. The result of complete co-operation on the part of railways and users was shown by such improvements as that from 24.7 tons average load per freight car to 33 tons between 1939 and 1943, due to a firm policy of full loading, despite all inconvenience. Efficiency of operation was responsible for the fact that this great effort was achieved with fewer locomotives, fewer freight cars, and only a slight increase in the number of passenger cars over what were used in 1917 for the very much smaller requirements of the first world war. Locomotive service was admirable, and steam locomotives were so well maintained and operated that regular through workings included Montreal to Halifax (840 miles) and Winnipeg to Jasper (1,030 miles). The war years truly saw the railways of Canada performing at their very best.

CHAPTER 13

Post-War Years: 1946-71

B efore turning to the extremely serious problems that faced the railways from the early fifties onwards, a brief glance may well be taken at what good rail travel used to be for the people of Canada and for those who visited their shores. Photographs make very clear how much heavier Canadian passenger cars are than those used in Europe. One had, however, only to see a long-distance train arrive from a journey through a bad blizzard, the locomotive coated with ice and snow and the under frames of every vehicle a solid mass of ice, to realise that any effort to economise in this direction would be of doubtful value—as has been found in practice. (Picture, p 143.) The heavy cars were comfortable for riding, despite all difficulties of track maintenance in spring time (when the 'frost comes out of the ground'). Individual coal (or later oil) stoves could still be found in passenger cars on isolated branch lines but engine steam heat generally maintained most comfortable conditions even in the depth of winter. On long-distance trains a 'news agent' (some of whom were characters right out of the pages of a book) would come through all the coaches (but not the sleepers) at regular intervals selling sandwiches and beverages. Pillows were provided at a small charge for some ease in sleeping.

Sleeping cars were, however, well provided on all overnight trains with accommodation at quite reasonable rates. There were usually three choices—a lower berth, an upper berth (cheaper but requiring more agility to get in), or the private bedroom, if one could afford it. The ingenious arrangement whereby the two berths were formed by letting down a folding section of the car ceiling, then sliding two facing seats together, all connected with appropriate gadetry and both enclosed by a long green curtain giving reasonable privacy, will be familiar to many readers if only because of the use of sleeping cars in many North American films of an earlier day. *Some Like It Hot* was a popular comedy film that showed the regular sleeping-car facilities to advantage even though cocktail parties in upper berths were not encountered frequently. Each car was presided over by a porter, usually a dark-skinned Canadian; these men seemed to be a fixture on the Canadian railway scene. They had a difficult job which they always seemed to do well, many becoming fast friends with regular travellers, some proving on acquaintance to be delightful and homely philosophers with a rare insight into human foibles. Two communal washrooms served each car, each with four or five washbasins and all necessary fittings. One of the many delights of earlier train travel were contacts made while washing, surprise meetings when occupants gradually left the privacy of their green enclosures, and even the remarkable esprit-de-corps that governed all use of washrooms, each user being in honour bound to leave spotless the bowl he had used, a civilised practice sadly lacking today even in the most expensive air travel.

Bedrooms provided more luxurious accommodation if used by one or two, with private toilet facilities, but one paid for this privilege. They suffered from their location in the cars, being closer to the wheels than any of the regular berths, but this did not seem to affect their popularity with wealthy travellers. At one of the famous conversaziones of the Institution of Civil Engineers in London, in pre-war days, there was exhibited a special bed, the frame of which had been fitted with cams and geared drive so that it would vibrate in exactly the same manner as the cars of a Canadian transcontinental train. It was designed for a famous shipbuilder who made regular trans-Canada journeys in a railway bedroom. Some of his staff had the pleasure of making this same journey with suitable instruments for measuring the exact nature of the car movements, to be used in the design of the bed, the reason being that the owner of the bed found that Canadian trains were the only sleeping places that cured his insomnia. The writer saw the bed and heard the story but has never been able to get some of his younger friends, air travellers all, to believe it.

It could have been that the relief from office pressures and the regular exercise that almost all transcontinental travellers used to get at divisional points were the real reasons for the good sleep. The regular routine was a pleasant experience, divisional points being spaced at intervals of about 150 miles, stops for locomotive and train servicing being usually from twenty to thirty minutes, time enough to get a good constitutional up and down the long wooden platforms. There was always a refreshment room at each divisional point where sandwiches and other snacks could be obtained by those who did not wish to use the dining car. There was often a mad rush for the counter, but always time enough for all to be served, based on long experience. Stories of these rooms are legion, such as the case of the distinguished but very economically-minded scientist who, having to cross Canada with all his expenses paid, was so shocked by what he thought were the high prices in the dining car at his first meal that he made the entire journey (of three and a half days) existing on sandwiches and soft drinks, and lived to tell the tale, with keen delight.

Dining-car service was outstanding, always being of the first order. Since complete meals would have to be served through two days or more, with some supplies for emergencies (snowdrifts sometimes impeding the most important trains), the organisation of the kitchen cars was almost a work of genius. Some of the busiest diners in North America used to be those on the late afternoon Montreal-Toronto service, the writer once being told by the steward on duty that they would have served 240 dinners by the end of the run. No intoxicating liquor could be served due to provincial legislation, its appearance on 'common carriers' being a more recent development in Canada. But the parlour or club cars that were usually marshalled at the rear of the mainline trains provided most comfortable surroundings for relaxed enjoyment of the scenery or one's fellow travellers, special observation cars being attached for the journey through the mountains on the main transcontinental services.

On trains such as these, with excellent service, one could travel not only between Montreal and Toronto but also between all the major cities of eastern Canada; Montreal and Ottawa, and Ottawa and Toronto were two such important services. Between Montreal and Quebec City, CPR ran a series of named trains that had a character all their own, their dining-car service being unrivalled. Patronage in summer months dropped off when it was possible to make this 180 mile journey on a most comfortable overnight boat, yet another convenience in travel that has now disappeared. To cross Canada by train was an unforgettable experience—the first day amid the Precambrian lake and forest country, the next day across the rolling (not flat!) prairie lands, then a day through the majestic scenery of the mountains. Canadian Pacific did its 2,881 mile run in 87 hours 10 minutes; Canadian National had 2,930 miles to cover, but with its much easier grades its overall time was only very slightly longer. Travellers who were wise would go west over the CPR line and return over the CNR line, thus getting a variety of scenery and, if railway-minded, a vivid impression of the differences in operating the two lines due to the CN's use of the Yellowhead Pass. At Vancouver, one could board a splendid CPR steamer directly from the station and steam across to Victoria, overnight or during the day, a stay at the famous Empress Hotel being a fitting climax to this great journey. 'Afternoon Tea at the Empress' was and is a ritual that is famous throughout Canada.

From Vancouver, there were convenient rail connections across the border to Seattle, and so by US lines down to California and across the States to the east. At Winnipeg, one could travel south similarly to St Paul-Minneapolis, and thence to Chicago with its multiplicity of connections. The main US links from Toronto were provided by the Toronto, Hamilton & Buffalo Railway (a subsidiary of the CPR and the NYCRR) giving connections at Buffalo with many mainline trains. Through trains from Toronto to Chicago have already been mentioned; they were well used by eastern Canadians travelling to the mid-west and the US west coast. From Montreal, one of the truly famous international trains, the Montrealer of the Delaware & Hudson Railroad, provided splendid overnight service to New York, the make-up being often more than a dozen sleeping cars. There were even direct US connections from Quebec City using the Quebec Central Railway (another CPR subsidiary) through Sherbrooke to junctions with the CP and CN lines to Boston and New England. CNR for many years ran a through night sleeper from Montreal to Washington DC, via New York, using the lines of the Boston & Maine and New Haven railroads in New England for its approach to New York, and the Pennyslvania Railroad thence to Washington. And from Saint John, there was a regular service to the south across the international border at Vanceboro and so to connections with the railways of Maine with links to the rest of the US rail system.

There were international links in the other direction also, one of the most interesting being a branch of the NYCRR from Malone, across the St Lawrence at Cornwall and up to Ottawa. Chartered originally in 1882 as the Ontario Pacific Railway; it was then reorganised in 1897 as the Ottawa & New York Railway; it was absorbed into the predecessor of the NYCRR in 1913. Although it once did provide through service from Ottawa to US points, it has now disappeared, the track having been removed in 1958, the right-of-way planned for use as yet another major highway. Service on branch-line trains such as those on this US spur to Ottawa had a charm all their own. In more isolated districts, they provided a link between communities that had a quite endearing character. All who travelled the Gaspé branch line in winter, for example, when roads would be blocked with snow, can recall the exchange of local news around the stove at the end of each car as new passengers got aboard at successive small settlements. Local service on the DAR, along the north coast of Nova Scotia, was similar, although with the CPR boat connection at Digby the connecting trains had the dignity of a combined dining-club car. The writer will never forget a journey on this pleasant train on a summer day in the late thirites. As the train approached the lovely little National Park at Grand Pré, where Evangeline is memorialised, it came slowly to a halt far from the station. The porter leaned over the rear of the club car and received his daily gift of fresh flowers from the gardener in the little park, flowers that soon graced his few dining tables. Such pleasures have, alas, gone for ever, and it is to the austere post-war changes in Canadian railroading that attention must now be directed.

Post-war adjustments were difficult everywhere but nowhere more so than on the railways of Canada. The tremendous freight and passenger loads created by wartime demand quickly dropped off. Following shortly thereafter was the loosening of the pent-up demand for 'consumer goods' including private automobiles. Wartime buses and trucks had shown what good service they could provide using the highway system that had done such yeoman service throughtout the war. And the development of flying throughout the war showed what potential existed in the modest services then provided by Trans-Canada Airlines, a publicly-financed airline that was created by the government of Canada in 1936, on the initiative of the Hon C. D. Howe, previously a consulting engineer of note and Canada's unofficial Deputy Prime Minister throughout the war years, and beyond. And beyond all these portents of things to come, the Canadian railways were still plagued with a freight-rate structure that was in many ways the lowest in the world, and remarkably inflexible.

Just as railway managements were grappling with these difficult problems in 1950, the railway unions called a strike that affected all Canadian lines. It lasted only nine days but in many ways it was one of the most unfortunate labour disputes in Canadian history. There have been longer and more troublesome strikes on Canadian railways since then but none that had such a profound effect on their future. Shippers of urgently needed goods, and especially of perishable materials, were driven into the arms of the trucking industry. It responded manfully, giving surprisingly good service at short notice. Many companies used trucks for the first time; many never went back to railway service. The decline of the railways of Canada from their unrivalled position as the dominant factor in transportation may well be dated from 1950. Many and complex factors were at work in changing the long-held position of the railways but the nine-day strike of 1950 certainly acted as a lamentable accelerator.

Both major railways were already busy with plans for increasing their efficiency and for active competition for business. A major change was the replacement of steam locomotives with diesel power. Although a few small shunting engines provided a link with the pioneering diesel experiments of CNR in the late twenties, it was not until the immediate post-war years that serious attention was given to the potential that diesel-powered locomotives provided, especially in view of steadily increasing labour costs. Both major Canadian companies were experimenting with mainline diesels as early as 1949. In that year the CPR used diesel locomotives for its overnight Montreal to Boston service. One of the first CNR's extensive changes was on Prince Edward Island where diesels replaced steam locomotives completely in 1950. It was in October 1954 that the first public announcement of diesel locomotive working for transcontinental trains was made. This followed many months of trials, then of diesel working (on the CP) from Montreal to Calgary. Once introduced, the multiple diesel units started working all the way through from Montreal to Vancouver, distances of 2,881 and 2,930 miles respectively, for CP and CN, world records for through operation of locomotives that are still unbeaten.

Operating experiences of the winter of 1953–54 were well recorded and put to dramatic use when both railways announced (in February 1955) their summer schedules, as usual, for introduction when summertime came into general use on 24 April. Cross-country times were drastically reduced, by sixteen and fourteen hours, respectively, (CP and CN), surely the largest reductions in running times for individual trains ever made in one step. But, in addition, the CPR announced that they were introducing on that day an entirely new suite of trains. The new service was to be called The Canadian, and would be diesel-hauled with all streamlined stainless steel coaches, including dome cars in every train. The publicity surrounding this bold venture was rightly widespread. The train justified everything that was said about it, and remains one of the very finest complete trains ever to operate in North America. CNR replied with the Super-Continental, an equally splendid train incorporating fine new stock but without the somewhat glamourised appearance that the stainless-steel finish gave to the CP trains and without the quickly popular dome cars for observation.

The dramatic reduction in overall running times was obtained by greater speeds, necessitating much track improvement, but more particularly by a great reduction in the length of station stops at divisional points, engine servicing now being required less frequently. In order to give passengers the best possible scenic views, departure and arrival times had also to be completely changed; it took regular travellers and residents of smaller towns on the routes a little time to become adjusted to such drastic departures from what had 'always' been the transcontinental train times. Operation of both diesel and steam locomotives was not economical or convenient; the inevitable result was obvious for all to see but few expected the completion of the changeover to come so quickly. The accompanying graph depicts the rapidity of the change. The last regularly-scheduled steam-operated train on CNR was that from The Pas to Winnipeg on 25 April 1960, a regular working. CPR made their last steam train operation (apart from one month more for steam operation of Montreal commuter trains) on 1 May 1960, a special occasion when they ran an excursion train from Toronto to Orangeville,

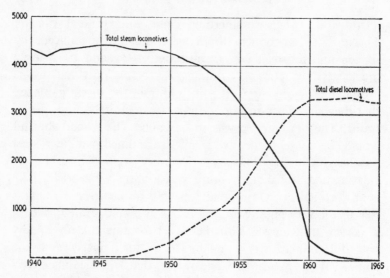

Fig 3: Steam to diesel transition on Canadian Railways

fifty miles away up a steeply graded line that gave railway photographers great scope as the three locomotives heading the 14-car train (with one thousand railway enthusiasts aboard) breasted the steep grades for the last time.

CNR continued to keep a few of their steam locomotives in operating order, one—the justly famous No 6218—until July 1971, but in effect the summer of 1960 saw the end of the steam era throughout Canada. Much was said about the economies that diesel locomotives would introduce but no figures appear to have been published to substantiate this claim. The capital loss incurred by the retirement of almost five thousand excellent steam locomotives in about ten years is difficult to appreciate as an 'economy measure', as is also the admittedly shorter working lives of diesel-electric units. All diesel locomotives for Canadian use have been purchased like automobiles from one or other of the major manufacturers, the long tradition of locomotive building at Angus shops and at Pointe St Charles being yet another casualty. Operating experience has been generally satisfactory, although initially CNR had much trouble with a special problem on its more isolated lines such as the NTR route in northern Ontario. The air-actuated horns on the diesels that first replaced steam whistles unfortunately were said to sound exactly the same as the mating call of the moose. A number of these fine animals were killed by the trains, the calls from which had attracted them. The tone of the horns had to be considerably changed.

Management problems, however, were the most serious that had ever faced the senior executives of the railways of Canada. The rapid advance of automotive highway transport dominated the transport picture in Canada from the early fifties onwards, just as it did in so many other countries, notably the United States. A further development affecting passenger transport was the remarkable development of Air Canada (Trans-Canada Airlines renamed in 1964) into one of the major airlines of the world, giving excellent and frequent service to all the populated parts of Canada, supplemented by the corresponding but more limited service of Canadian Pacific Airlines, after its formation from a group of small companies in 1942. The airlines skimmed off the cream of long-distance passenger travel and have now taken over almost all transport of mail, the last run of a railway postal car having taken place in April 1971. Trucking companies have similarly skimmed off the cream of the packet freight business and in some instances have undertaken carriage of bulk freight to the disadvantage of railways. Pipelines, of which there are now more than 6,000 miles in operation in Canada, are carrying not only natural gas but also most of the oil that might have been valuable freight for railway haulage, amounting to 20 per cent of all freight. It has been the private automobile that has had the most spectacular effect on passenger rail travel, however, there being now a large number of young Canadians who have never even been in a train, let along enjoyed a long distance journey, the 'family car' being their invariable means of transport.

These are problems which are not peculiar to Canada but they have affected Canadian railways more seriously than those of most other countries, if only because of the many services that the railways must provide, irrespective of whether they are enjoying their full share of the transport business or not. Operation of both major railways across the 'thousand-mile gap' north of Lake Superior is but one example of the special geographic and economic difficulties of railway operation in Canada. Despite all these difficulties, managements of the two major railways, and of the two dozen still independent small lines, have made valiant attempts to meet the problems and to maintain and improve their systems as particularly vital parts of the Canadian transport network. Nevertheless, the unique position that the railways occupied until the years of the second world war has been lost, never to be regained.

The problems continue; so, also, do the active efforts of railway management to improve their efficiency and to attract and retain business. Permanent way has been steadily improved and well maintained on all main lines, using mechanical equipment to such a degree that the number of men necessary has been greatly reduced. Centralised train control systems are now common throughout Canada instead of being the exception; signalling on most of the important main lines is now by three-aspect colour lights, the combination of these two features mitigating to a degree the inherent restraints of single-line working. New equipment for both passenger and freight traffic has been introduced on an extensive scale, such items as triple-deck automobile carriers, complete 'piggy-back' trains between major cities, and the use of a wide variety of containers being now commonplace.

The present position of the private automobile in Canada is indicated by the fact that the country now has considerably more such automobiles than there are individual households. Even before the war, automobiles accounted for well over 60 per cent of all inter-city passenger miles. There was a natural drop during the war, but the position had been restored by 1949, thence to go on improving until today private cars account for more than 85 per cent of all inter-city mileage. Trans Canada Highway, a splendid paved road built to modern high standards, stretches from coast to coast. Between major cities in the east, great divided highways now permit speedy travel, many Canadians thinking little of driving the 350 miles from Montreal to Toronto, on the leading such highway, in only part of a day.

The remaining 15 per cent of inter-city travel is divided between railways, buses and airlines in approximately equal parts. Bus travel, surprisingly in a way, has been seriously affected also by the inroads of the private automobile, passengers dropping from an all-time high of 145 million in 1949 to below 60 million in the late sixties. Passenger travel by air has increased spectacularly. Passenger miles increased from 132 million to over 1,000 million in the decade from 1945 to 1955, and now exceed four billion. One might expect this to be mainly in long-distance travel but such is the attraction of flying for younger Canadians that the 'triangle route' (Montreal-Ottawa-Toronto) is Air Canada's busiest service. Only when the weather is bad do devoted air travellers ever think of trains; they then expect to get, at no notice, exactly the same service that they received in pre-flying days. The railways do their best, and sometimes seem to work miracles, but the weather clears, and they are again forgotten after being blamed by the unthinking for their poor service!

The freight situation is just as serious for the railways but considerably less complicated. Straight competition with alternative modes of transport is here the key to survival, cost and convenience (such as door-to-door delivery by truck) being the main determinants. Table 3 shows the essential facts for selected years, starting from the last normal pre-war year. The great overall increase will be first noted; all individual totals have similarly increased even though the various percentage shares of the total traffic have changed considerably. The relative situation of the railways, compared with the situation in 1938, has not changed to nearly the same extent as with passenger traffic. Water traffic still looms large on the Canadian scene, mainly because of the Great Lakes shipping services now with a direct outlet to the sea through the St Lawrence

TABLE 3: Total Ton Miles of Freight Movements in Canada

(All figures are ton-miles × 000,000)

Year	Rail	%	Water	%	Road	%	Air	%	Pipeline	%	Total
1938	26,835	51.0	24,267	46.1	1,515	2.9	1	—	—	—	52,618
1945	63,349	71.7	21,994	25.0	2,995	3.3	3	—	—	—	88,341
1950	55,538	60.1	27,017	29.2	9,240	10.0	8	—	610	0.7	92,413
1955	66,176	52.1	34,348	27.0	13,750	10.8	31	—	12,820	10.1	127,125
1961	65,828	36.6	61,430	34.2	17,990	10.0	45	—	34,400	19.2	179,693
1964	86,974	37.4	78,020	33.6	19,490	8.4	64	—	47,830	20.6	232,378
1967	94,100	37.0	76,640	30.1	21,720	8.5	130	—	62,290	24.4	254,880

Source: *Canada: 1867–1967* p 215—a special centenary edition of the annual abridgement of the *Canada Year Book* (Dominion Bureau of Statistics) with additions and revisions from Statistics Canada, 1972).

Seaway. Trucking made spectacular gains after the war years but its peak seems to have passed, even though the trucking industry, in Canada as elsewhere, continues to be active and aggressive in competition. The railways are more than holding their own, after their low year of 1961. This is due to the keen efforts of both major railways but also to the spectacular increases, even though small in total volume, on some of the smaller railways of Canada, to the development of which attention will shortly be directed.

Passenger traffic on the railways of Canada today will be of prime interest to readers. From a total of almost thirty million passengers in 1941, passenger business had increased to over sixty million in 1944, such were the demands upon railway service at the peak of wartime activity. Traffic quickly dropped to the thirty million level again by 1950, but went on dropping to an all-time low (for recent years) of less than ninteen million in 1961, since when there has been a slight increase up to the twenty million level, with a peak of almost twenty-seven million in 1967. This was the year of Canada's Centenary when the many attractions arranged, notably EXPO '67 in Montreal, induced a great deal of extra travel much of it by rail, extra transcontinental services even being run during that happy summer.

CNR are almost wholly responsible for the maintenance of Canadian railroad passenger traffic. They pioneered the introduction into North America of a new varied fare system, using the concept of 'red, and blue and white days' each colour indicating a different fare structure depending on the normal amount of traffic on that day. 'Red days', for example, are usually mid-week days when traffic is light; 'white days', on the other hand, are usually Sundays and Fridays, 'blue days' being holidays and other periods of unusually heavy normal traffic. This scheme has attracted an appreciable amount of business back to CNR trains, as have such changes as including the price of meals in ticket costs, following airline practice. Beyond all this, however, is the spirit of progress that CNR management have induced in all their staff who deal with passengers. It is perhaps safe to say that the future of North American passenger rail travel depends to a large extent on the success that meets these CNR efforts in the years immediately ahead. The position that CNR now occupies in the North American railway passenger scene is well shown by a comparison of the published timetables, current as this book goes to press, for CNR, CPR and AMTRAK (the nationally-financed combination of almost all USA lines still carrying any passengers). This is shown in Table 4.

TABLE 4: Comparative Study of North American
Railroad Timetables

Rail System	CNR	CPR	AMTRAK
Date of Issue	31 October 1971	31 October 1971	16 January 1972
Pages (excl. of covers)	24	10	70 (c)
Index, Fares, Adverts etc	9	2	49
Nett Timetable pages	15	8	21
'Daily' Trains (a)	104	30	102 + 98 (d)
Other Trains (b)	65	14	18
RR Bus Services	31	16	—
RR Steamer Services	6	10	—

Notes: (a) Operating five, six, or seven consecutive days each week
     (b) Sundays only, Saturdays and Sundays, or three alternate days each week
     (c) Size explained by inclusion of 'airline' simplified schedules and duplication of many trains
     (d) 102 trains between Boston-New York-Philadelphia-Washington, 98 Amtrak trains for the rest of the USA

All indications are that CPR management would be most happy to see no passenger service left on what was once the pride of Canada as 'the world's greatest travel system'. For almost a decade, regular travellers have had to witness, always with regret, very obvious efforts on the part of the CPR to discourage passengers from using their trains, the climax coming when the company requested permission from the Canadian Transport Commission to discontinue operating The Canadian. The reasons are clear. Operating passenger facilities is a nuisance; operating long freight trains with multiple-diesel units is a much more profitable business, and this the CPR continues to do extremely well as shown by its recent financial performance for shareholders' benefit. It has now contracted to deliver large quantities of coal from the east slopes of the Rockies to Vancouver for shipment to Japan; it must be most annoying to operating personnel to have to give The Canadian (with its few passengers in winter) priority over these great 100-car trains operating over the single track up and down those appalling grades through the mountains. (Picture, p 126.) The story is such a sad one from the point of view of railway travellers that it will be best to draw a veil across the history of the last few years of CPR passenger service beyond recording, without comment, that the familiar beaver insignia, known around the world, has now been replaced by a modern public relations firm's gimmick, and that at the time of the annual meeting of the Canadian Pacific Railway Co on 1 May 1971 this great and famous name was abolished, being replaced by 'Canadian Pacific Limited', rail operations being now designated as 'CPRail'.

The Canadian Transport Commission has just been mentioned. This regulatory body, with very wide powers, was established in 1967 and took the place of previous separate boards for each of the main forms of transport. Its establishment was in line with the main recommendations of yet another Royal Commission, appointed in 1959 to study all forms of transport in Canada. Headed by Mr Justice Macpherson, its three-volume report was issued between 1961 and 1962, and reflected in the National Transportation Act of 1967. The Canadian Transport Commission operates through six major committees, each chaired by one of the commissioners; one naturally deals with rail transport. To the commission, through this committee, the railways of Canada may now apply for relief from the financial burden of uneconomical passenger services. The commission may decide that a service shall be discontinued or if it should be maintained in the public interest, in which case compensatory payment may be made to the railway concerned by the Government of Canada. A complex procedure involving five major steps has been established through which the public interest is safeguarded but the term 'uneconomic' naturally depends upon the accounting systems that are used. These are also subject to commission control even though they may be far beyond the ordinary passenger's knowledge or comprehension. Both major railways have not hesitated to utilise these procedures to the full. In the hands of the Canadian Transport Commission, therefore, rests much of the responsibility for future rail passenger service in Canada.

CHAPTER 14

Lines to the North: 1899-1971

The general pattern of railway development in Canada has been, quite naturally, from east to west, public thinking about railways still being dominated by thoughts of the building of the great transcontinental lines. A network of branch lines existed in almost all parts of the country, well covering that narrow strip north of the Canadian-US border in which almost the whole of the population of the country resides. Familiar also were the south-bound connections with the railway system of the United States so briefly summarised on p 178. All that has been said about the problems of Canadian railways applied to all these lines. Many branch lines have been removed. Nationalisation of passenger services in the USA has cut most of the previously important rail connections between the two countries. There is, however, one further chapter in the history of railways in Canada that is full of excitement and challenge, this being the service now given by lines running to the north, rather than the south, into the still wild parts of the Dominion where no roads yet run. Existing lines have been rehabilitated with improved services, new lines have been built, and are still being built. Even though the mileage involved is not very great by transcontinental standards, the importance of these lines to the economy of Canada, and their special interest to all who enjoy railways, warrants this summary review. They are to be found from east to west of the country, and in the very far north; small-scale maps can therefore merely indicate their location.

Labrador, a part of the province of Newfoundland, and

eastern Quebec, occupying the eastern part of the great area of eastern Canada capped by the Ungava peninsula, have been well described as 'the Land that God gave Cain' so desolate and inhospitable a place is it, much of it bare rock, much underlain by ground that is perennially frozen. This condition is known as 'permafrost', and it underlies about one-half the land area of Canada. If the ground consists of water-bearing soil, as is often the case near rivers and lakes, the water will be ice. Any disturbance of the protecting cover of muskeg, as by construction operations, will allow this ice to melt in summer months, often with disastrous results since the soil and water usually flow like soup.

Small bands of Indians ranged the Labrador plateau, coming to the coast for supplies in summer, but even they avoided some areas where compasses had long ago been found to be useless. Iron ore was the cause of this phenomenon; it was first reported in 1895 by A. P. Low, a great geologist-explorer, but not until 1936 was any move made to explore the ore potential. In 1942-3 the Hollinger Mining Co gained control of the exploration company that had then been formed. It was soon found that iron ore of good quality was present in vast quantities, but over three hundred miles from the nearest coast. In 1947, therefore, there was formed the Quebec, North Shore & Labrador Railway, now a subsidiary of the Iron Ore Co of Canada which, in turn, was formed in 1949. In 1950 a small freighter landed the first construction equipment at the tiny port of Seven Islands and work started on a 350-mile railway in incredibly difficult country, and the transformation of the little wharf at Sept-Iles, Quebec, into a modern shipping terminal capable of handling ten million tons of ore a year.

The line rises to an elevation of 2,066 ft at mileage 150 but then descends to the general level of the plateau at about 1,700 ft above sea level. Since almost all freight movement is southward, ruling grades are 1.35 per cent going north, and 0.4 per cent coming south to the coast. The most difficult section for construction was up the gorge-like valley of the Moisie

River; here two tunnels, 2,200 and 1,050 ft long, and a major bridge were necessary. Total length of the main line is 356 miles. In 1960 a 36-mile branch into the Carol mining area was completed but traffic had already been operating on the main line since 31 July 1954 when the first train load of ore left Schefferville, the mining town at the end of the line. This is an entirely new community with a population of over 4,000; Sept-Iles, the shipping port, has a population of over 20,000. When the writer visited this location in 1937, the total population, including visiting Montaignais Indians, was at most two hundred, the magnificent harbour formed by the Bay of Seven Islands visited only occasionally by small coastal vessels. Today, some of the largest ore carriers in the world sail into this same bay to take their share of the millions of tons of iron ore shipped annually, some up into the Great Lakes, some south to east-coast US ports, some across the Atlantic. A maximum daily shipment of 110,000 tons has been achieved. All this comes down the railroad which is equipped with 2,977 ore cars, each carrying 85 long tons; 600 miscellaneous and passenger cars (there being a thrice-weekly passenger service, despite general reliance upon air travel); with seventy-seven 1,750 hp mainline diesels and six rated at 3,000 hp. Centralised traffic control is exercised from Sept-Iles, normal trains consisting of 135 cars with multiple-units for haulage, fifteen hours being taken for the southbound trip, fourteen hours for the northbound empty run, limiting speeds being 30 and 40 mph, respectively. During construction of the great Churchill Falls power project to the east of the railroad, all major freight was brought into Sept-Iles and shipped northward on the railway to a small stop called Esker where it was unloaded, to complete its journey over a specially built highway running east to the construction site.

A map will show how isolated this important and busy railway is apart only from the parallel Cartier Railroad, 190 miles long from Port Cartier to similarly large iron ore deposits at Lac Jeannine, opened in 1962. Some 250 miles to the west, there is another industrial line joining the deep-water port of Bagotville, at the end of Ha! Ha! Bay near the head of tidewater in the great Saguenay River, with the Arvida plant of the Aluminium Co of Canada (also with the CNR line from Quebec). Opened in 1925, this short line hauls the bauxite ore required for this largest of all aluminium plants from the wharf to which ocean-going vessels deliver it, as well as other bulk freight. One of Canada's strangest railways, however, once existed in much closer proximity to Sept-Iles, this being a 25-mile long logging railway constructed in 1909–10 on Anticosti Island. This 120-mile long by 30-mile wide island is still used only for logging operations, with some hunting and fishing. Once owned by the Menier interests of France, it then saw its most active period of development, the railway being once evidence of this. Three small locomotives were brought in; the line was operated for about ten years but it has long since almost disappeared, only a few signs remaining today of this pioneer venture.

Many other small railways were built to assist logging operations in the forests of Canada, especially in British Columbia, far too many to record here. A number are in operation today, all now converted to diesel operation, even though massive automotive transporters and huge trucks have taken over much of this specialised transport. Two logging railways are still in active operation, surprisingly, in eastern Canada. From the small town of Thurso, thirty miles east of Ottawa on the north bank of the Ottawa River, the Thurso & Nation Valley Railway, originally built in 1925 by the Singer Sewing Machine Co, runs northward for fifty-eight miles into beautiful hardwood forests. The company used this wood for making the cabinets for their machines but sold the property in 1964 to a pulp and paper company which operates a pulp mill, and the original furniture mill, at Thurso. A diesel-hauled daily train brings logs from the forests, the service it provides being still competitive with possible road haulage. Far to the north-west is the pleasant company town of Kapuskasing, located on the former National Transcontinental line west of Cochrane. Here is the large paper mill of the

Spruce Falls Power & Paper Co, jointly owned by the Kimberley Clark Corporation and the *New York Times*, supplying the newsprint for this famous newspaper. Power for the mill comes from the Smoky Falls power plant, fifty miles to the north, constructed in 1923 with the aid of a specially built private railway up from Kapuskasing. After carrying all the freight needed for the power plant, the line was used for lumber haulage and has continued in this service ever since. In 1971 a steam-powered special passenger train was operated on it as part of the fiftieth anniversary celebration of this fine northern town.

Had a stop been made at Cochrane, another railway would have been seen coming up from the south, this being one of the true pioneer lines of the north, now known as the Ontario Northland Railway (ONR). As early as 1884, with completion of the Canadian Pacific Railway in prospect, there were visionaries who saw the railway as a means of opening up the clearly valuable farming land in northern Ontario, to the west of Lake Temiskaming and to the north of the new railway town of North Bay. It was not until 1900, however, that the Ontario Legislature voted $40,000 for surveys of a possible line north. In 1902 an Act was passed establishing the Temiskaming and Northern Ontario (TNOR) Railway as a provincially-owned company. (Although railway charters were usually granted by the Government of Canada, there was nothing to stop a province taking such an action provided that its railway did not cross its own boundaries.) Construction started in the same year; from the start it was plagued with difficulties but, by 1904, steel had reached Englehart (139.8 miles). Cochrane (253.6 miles) was reached in 1908 but before this a spectacular find of silver ore had been made near Cobalt (104.1 miles) in one of the rock cuttings necessary for the railway. This started a mining boom comparable, except in degree, with the Klondyke gold rush, first for silver ore, then for gold in the Kirkland Lake, Noranda and Timmins areas, many of the mines then started being still active producers today.

The fortunes of the pioneer 'colonisation' railway changed almost overnight; from the outset it has been an important mover of valuable freight to and from the mines. Most fortunately, it had purchased in 1911 the small electric railway between Haileybury and Cobalt, the Nipissing Central Railway, which operated under a federal charter. By means of this charter, it was able to build in 1927 a branch line across its boundary into Noranda, Quebec, and so to obtain some of the business from this important mining area, sharing this with CNR which had previously reached Rouyn-Noranda by means of a long loop line off the NTR line between Senneterre and Taschereau. In 1922, the main line was extended northward from Cochrane, as had always been the dream, but only for 44.4 miles to serve the construction of a large water-power plant in Abitibi River canyon. Only in 1932 was the final stage to the shore of James Bay (the south end of Hudson Bay) achieved, the main line being then 440 miles long. This last section was really built as an unemployment relief measure since the railway stops by a muddy shore, its terminal, called Moosonee, being across the Moose River from the old trading post of Moose Factory. But a service has been provided continuously even to this isolated location on Arctic waters, in recent years at an increasing frequency for tourists and nature lovers. For a brief period much freight was taken into Moosonee for the construction of adjacent posts on the Mid-Canada radar defence line. And there are naturally still those who dream of Moosonee one day becoming another great ocean port.

Headquarters of the railway are at North Bay. The line had to change its name, regrettably, in 1946 because of confusion with the reporting marks of the Texas & New Orleans Railroad; since the TNOR came first alphabetically, it used regularly to receive bills intended for the southern line. The Ontario Northland Railway, therefore, it then became and continues so to this day, now operating an extensive bus passenger service through its territory, as well as its own excellent passenger train service and a communications system that is invaluable to the northern communities it links. The ONR also operates summer boat services on Lakes Nipissing and Temagami, the latter still a wild and lovely place. In its history it has served many mines, some now long closed down, and assisted with massive freight haulage for construction projects, notably of water-power plants on the rivers of the north.

Possibly its peak of service was when the new Continental Limited train of the newly formed CNR used the TNOR main line from North Bay to Cochrane in order to reach the NTR line as an alternative to use of the Long Lac Cut-Off. The writer had the pleasure of using this service when making journeys between Montreal and Cobalt in 1929 and 1930 while serving as resident engineer on one of the power plants just mentioned, the only access to which was over the Silver Centre TNOR branch from Cobalt, a branch line long since taken up. He can testify to the excellent service in those difficult days given by this provincially-owned railway. It was one of the first Canadian lines to convert completely to diesel motive power, the last steam locomotive being retired in June 1957. Today it is served by twenty mainline diesel units and twenty-three smaller units, all finished in an unusually smart livery. Its progressive character is well shown by the success of its Polar Bear Express from Cochrane to Moosonee. Now requiring fourteen coaches during summer months, this train is scheduled to permit of return within the day to Cochrane, giving hundreds of Canadians every year an easy opportunity of setting foot on their Arctic coastline. But it operates also three times a week throughout the winter, providing a vital link to the settlers in this lonely area, still untouched by roads.

Two hundred and fifty miles to the west of North Bay is the important industrial centre of Sault Ste Marie, at the outlet from Lake Superior through the St Mary's River. Here starts yet another line to the north, this one privately-owned, also originally intended to reach the shores of James Bay. The Algoma Central Railway (ACR) parallels the ONR in that its name also was changed, but as late as 1965, from the Algoma Central & Hudson Bay Railroad Co, an admission of a changed viewpoint as to the railway's destiny. In the closing years of the last century a far-sighted industrialist, F. H. Clergue, organised a number of enterprises at 'The Soo' (to give the colloquial nickname). These have developed into a great steel complex, a paper company, a power company and the ACR, even though in the opening years of this century financial conditions were such that Mr Clergue lost control of his enterprises.

The railway was planned to link iron mines near the Michipicoten River with the mills at the Sault, with a branch to a harbour on Lake Superior. Clearing for this latter section was started as early as 1899. When the financial upheaval of 1903 took place, rails had reached nearly to Hawk Junction (56 miles) and from the new harbour fifteen miles up to the Helen Mine. In 1910 an English financial group obtained control of the Clergue interests and so construction was resumed, Hearst on the NTR line being reached in 1914. The country traversed in the southern section is the Precambrian Shield country at its most rugged. Aerial photography was not then available for assisting with route location, and the result was one of the most rugged lines to operate in eastern Canada. Grades up to $2\frac{1}{2}$ per cent have to be faced; the longest straight stretch is one of eight miles only; curvature is the equivalent of $87\frac{1}{2}$ complete circles with a maximum curvature of 13 degrees. So economical had the original construction to be that there were originally 204 wooden bridges and trestles; all but seven have now been replaced with steel, concrete or embankment fill.

Difficulties have been not only those of a difficult route; financial affairs, too, have had a chequered career so that it was only in 1959 that shareholders of the company again assumed control, since when it quickly became a financially profitable concern. It is the oldest Canadian bulk carrier on the Great Lakes and has an efficient and growing fleet of modern vessels carrying about six million tons of freight each year. The railway carries annually about four million tons, of which products of mines amount to about 60 per cent, forest products 16 per cent, the remainder being manufactured goods. The ACR has the unique distinction of crossing the main lines of both CNR (the old CNOR route) and the CPR at grade, at Oba and Franz, respectively, before reaching its terminal point at Hearst on the northern CNR line, these three connections giving fruitful interchanges of traffic. ACR was the first railway in Canada to go over to diesel haulage, steam being abandoned in 1952. Twenty-six diesels (1,500 and 1,700 hp) and two yard switchers make up its motive power; five units are often used on its heavy freights. It operates 1,813 freight cars and 135 miscellaneous and passenger cars, passenger service still being maintained between Sault Ste Marie and Hearst on a daily basis in summer months. And the ACR is building up also a summer tourist business, needing a steadily increasing number of air-conditioned cars for its summer excursion trains from the Sault up to the beautiful Agawa Canyon. (Picture, p 54.)

The Hudson Bay Railway (part of CNR) is probably Canada's best known northern line; rarely a year goes by without some press reference to the annual shipments of grain out of Hudson Bay, grain that has been brought from the prairies over this unique line to the port of Churchill. No sooner had the CPR been completed than agitation started for an outlet from the west by way of Hudson Bay. It was thought that this would reduce freight charges because of the substantial reduction in travel distance to Europe; it would also give a route out of the control of 'eastern Canadian interests'. It will be recalled that the original part of the CNOR was a small line that was intended to go to Hudson Bay (see p 112) but which stopped on the shores of Lake Winnepegosis. The CNOR later carried this line westward to Prince Albert in Saskatchewan but by 1911 it had put into operation a northern branch line from Hudson Bay Junction back into Manitoba as far as The Pas near latitude 54°N. This was as far as private interests went but the Government of Canada, in response to western demands, had started the construction of the necessary major bridge at The Pas over the Saskatchewan River in 1910. Shortly there-after construction of the line to Hudson Bay was started, over

500 miles away across wild and inhospitable country, all the northern part underlain by permafrost. By 1913, rail service was started to Scott, merely a point on the map fifty-six miles north of The Pas. The demands of war slowed up progress but by 1918, when work was stopped, track was within ninety miles of the mouth of the Nelson River. Here was the historical York Factory, so that it was an obvious location for the long hoped-for deep-water port.

Agitation for completion of the line continued in the west, the On-to-the-Bay Association being especially active. In 1926 the government decided to continue with construction but decision as to the port location was placed before Mr Frederick Palmer, a British consulting engineer, who recommended in 1927 that, despite the extra mileage, the port should be developed at the mouth of the Churchill River rather than the Nelson. This was accepted and plans adjusted accordingly. The track reached Churchill (509.8 miles from The Pas) on 29 March 1929 after quite remarkable construction difficulties with permafrost had been overcome. The port was developed with wharves, a large grain elevator, loading machinery and all necessary ancillary services, with the result that the first two cargoes of wheat were shipped to Europe from Hudson's Bay in September 1931.

At first a part of the Canadian Government Railways, the Hudson Bay Railway was placed under the federal Department of Railways and Canals in 1926 but was eventually passed to CNR for operation. Important branch lines have been built— to Lynn Lake for Sherridon (144 miles) in 1952–3 for mining; to Thompson (31 miles) in 1957 to serve the new town developed around a new nickel mine and refinery; and to Chisel Lake (52 miles) in 1958–59 also to assist with mining development. Wheat shipments are regularly made in ocean vessels during the short late-summer period of open navigation through Hudson Strait. And a regular passenger service is maintained summer and winter, the summer trains now attracting to Churchill tourists and nature lovers who want to 'get away from civilisation' but who must be most surprised when they first see the gaunt outline of the big grain elevator so close to the wind-swept Arctic tundra which comes right to the edge of the small settlement.

Since the main line of CNR lies relatively so far to the north, almost any branch line from it to the north could be classed as a 'northern line'. But only a few go into really undeveloped country. In northern Quebec, a great loop has been built to serve the Chibougamau mining area. In Alberta, a great network of lines serving what is known as the 'Peace River country' has been built, originally by three small private companies. The original lines were managed by the CPR in 1920 but later taken over by the provincial government, eventually being formed into the Northern Alberta Railways (NAR), bought and operated jointly by CPR and CNR. Strong demands came from residents of this fine farming country for an outlet to the Pacific coast and numerous studies were made. The outlet has now been provided by the next northern line to be mentioned. The most recent extension of this Alberta system, however, was built in 1964 by CNR from Roma in Alberta, 380 miles to Hay River on the shores of Great Slave Lake, north of the sixtieth parallel and so into the Northwest Territories of Canada. The new line, completed in 1965, roughly parallels a pioneer highway built a few years previously to Hay River, thence going on to Yellowknife, capital of the Territories. The railway, however, was constructed in order to provide transport to the outer world of the products of the important new lead-zinc mine at Pine Point, fifty miles east of Hay River on the south shore of the great lake (the fourth largest in North America). The only access prior to the new road and railway was either by air for passengers and light freight or down the Mackenzie waterway from the end of one of the NAR lines, running from Edmonton to Waterways on the Clearwater River at its junction with the Athabasca. The Pine Point line of CNR is therefore one of the truly pioneering railways into the north of Canada.

British Columbia is another province that owns a railway, but by default rather than by design. Despite its strange start, the Pacific Great Eastern Railway (PGER) has become one of Canada's most progressive smaller lines with a current record of new railway building unmatched in North America. At the peak of early railroad excitement, a provincial charter was granted in 1912 for the building of a railway from the vicinity of Vancouver 470 miles up Howe Sound and connecting valleys to Prince George on the new GTP line to Prince Rupert. The charter was granted to Messrs Foley, Welch and Stewart who were the contractors, but the capital came largely from British investors, associated with the Great Eastern Railway of England which contributed its name to the new line. The province guaranteed $4\frac{1}{2}$ per cent bonds to the amount of $42,000 per mile, or a total of about $20 million. Construction of the main line started at a small place called Squamish, at the head of the beautiful sound, an arm of the sea just to the north of the harbour of Vancouver, the city being forty miles away. A small start was also made at North Vancouver and about twelve miles of track were built, as far as Horseshoe Bay on Howe Sound but still almost thirty miles from Squamish; even this short line was difficult to maintain due to the mountain streams it crossed but a limited passenger service was provided from North Vancouver to the ferry at Horseshoe Bay using railcars. The depression of 1913, however, and the strains of war following 1914, soon put the contractors in difficulties; work had to stop; the province had to step in at the end of the war and take control of the property, continuing construction as far as Quesnel (344 miles), reached in 1921. There construction stopped and for the next twenty-eight years the isolated little line just existed, giving local service throughout the rugged terrain it served, the butt of sorry jokes, names such as 'Prince George Eventually' and 'Past God's Endurance' being popular explanations of 'PGE'.

In 1949, under a new provincial administration, a fresh start was made at upgrading the line and continuing it to Prince George, now well established as one of the growing communities of the B.C. 'interior'. Operations to Prince George, where connection was made with CNR, started in

January 1953. In August 1956 an even more important link was forged when a connection was completed from North Vancouver to Squamish and beyond, this 40-mile extension being one of the most difficult pieces of railway construction of this century, the line clinging to steep cliffs between a previously built road and the water's edge, as the picture on p 71 makes clear. Yards were developed at North Vancouver but motive power and service facilities remained at Squamish. The railway building continued; the Peace River country, on the other side of the Rockies, was reached in 1958. From Prince George the main line continues to Chetwynd, now an important junction, one line continuing on for sixty-nine miles to Fort St John, another sixty-one miles to Dawson Creek, just west of the B.C.-Alberta border, where connection is made with NAR. In 1966, a 23-mile spur was built to a completely new industrial town of Mackenzie; in 1968 the first seventy-eight miles of a new line going north up the Rocky Mountain Trench (a vast valley amid the mountains) was completed as far as Fort St James, the further 420-mile extension to Dease Lake being planned for completion in 1974. And the centenary of British Columbia in 1971 was duly celebrated by the ceremonial opening of a 250-mile extension from Fort St John to Fort Nelson.

The PGER, therefore, now has a mainline system well over 1,000 miles long; when Dease Lake is reached, it will be almost 1,800 miles in all. Its previous isolation has given way to connections with CNR and NAR as noted, and with both major railways at North Vancouver where it has now fine yard facilities, all line operations being controlled from its head office. It passes through some of the most splendid scenery of western Canada. From sea-level at Squamish, it reaches an altitude of 2,100 ft at Alta Lake, then drops in the next twenty-five miles to elevation 686 at Mount Currie. The Fraser River is crossed by the largest of the more than two hundred bridges on the line at mileage 121 from Squamish and at an elevation of 850 ft. Then the climbing starts again, to a height of 3,864 ft at Horse Lake, following which a switchback route leads down to Prince George at elevation 1,870. The entire main line is now laid with 100-lb rail. Discussions are said to have started with the idea of one day extending the PGER across the sixtieth parallel into the Yukon Territory. And as this book goes through the press its name is being changed to the British Columbia Railway.

A total of 3,620 freight cars are now in use, motive power being entirely diesel — sixteen 3,000 hp, two 2,000 hp, twenty-nine 1,800 hp, twenty-seven 1,600 hp, and four 1,000 hp. A daily passenger service giving a same-day return to Vancouver is now provided to Lillooet 157.7 miles from Vancouver; even this section of line goes up over 2,000 ft. On alternate days, a through service to Prince George is scheduled, all passenger service being given by six comfortable air-conditioned diesel railcars. The extension lines are still freight only; development of freight traffic shows what the PGER has done. Approximate numbers of car loadings have been as follows:

1950	12,000
1955	40,000
1960	65,000
1965	80,000
1970	115,000

It is no surprise to find that gross revenues have increased 50 per cent in the four years up to 1970. There must be few other comparable lines that can report a ten-fold increase in freight traffic in twenty years.

The railway has naturally been the beneficiary of the remarkable industrial development that has featured the province of British Columbia since the end of the war, and especially the interior region served by the PGER. There are now pulp and paper plants at Prince George, chemical plants and an oil refinery; two pulp mills at Mackenzie; a forest products terminal at Squamish, where there is also a new chemical plant; grain elevators at Dawson Creek, Taylor and Fort St John (in the Peace River country with its Pacific outlet at last); and an oil refinery and gas treatment plant at Taylor, this being in an area with potential for more petroleum product discoveries.

Despite these industrial plants, more than half the total freight carried consists of forest products, either in the raw or manufactured. Transport of steel pipes for the extensive oil and gas pipeline construction has been an important temporary load on the system. Of special interest has been the development of a 'piggy-back' service from Vancouver, some trucks so transported going on to the north up the Alaska Highway. It is impossible for a writer who can so clearly remember the quiet sad scenes at Squamish in the twenties and thirties to conceal his delight in what the PGER is now doing, fully justifying its modern popular name of 'Progressively Greater Earnings' to the benefit of the province that owns it and its people.

There is still yet one more northern line in Canada to be described, in many ways the most remarkable of all. It will be found on the map in the far north-west corner of Canada, its northern section north of the sixtieth parallel. It has been in continuous operation since 1900, never having received a subsidy from any government (an almost unique distinction) and always privately owned. This is the White Pass & Yukon Route (WPYR), a narrow gauge (3 ft) line, 110 miles long from tidewater at Skagway, Alaska, to Whitehorse, capital of the Yukon Territory. The Klondyke gold rush of 1897 attracted the attention of the whole world and still does, so remarkable were the adventures of those who managed to sail the 867 miles north from Vancouver to the head of the Lynn Canal (a deep fiord of the sea) landing at Skagway, making the terrific and terrible climb over the Chilkoot Pass, and surviving the dangers of the final sail down the Yukon River to the Klondyke area. There were other routes in but this was the one generally used so that Skagway became overnight a place of importance. It is said that it was in a bar there that Sir Thomas Tancred, representing English financial interests with the idea of building a railway over the pass, met Michael J. Heney, a Canadian with some railroad experience. They certainly met, the Englishman discouraged at the impossibility of ever building anything over the pass, Heney with courage, enthusiasm and the certainty that he could do it. It was this remarkable combination that achieved what so many regarded as quite impossible; construction started in April 1898 and the rails reached Whitehorse on 8 June 1900. The cost was said to be $10 million; as many as 35,000 men were at work at one time since the whole line was virtually built by hand.

Starting at sea level at Skagway, the line begins to climb almost as soon as the terminal yard is left, reaching the boundary between Canada and the USA at Summit Lake having climbed 2,900 ft in only twenty miles. Maximum grade is 3.9 per cent, the average for the twenty miles being 2.6 per cent, but the curvature is in places as much as 16°. (Picture, p 89.) The line follows a steadily mounting route along the steep mountain sides that lead up to the White Pass, discovered after the original Chilkoot Pass, making a long loop up a side valley in order to gain mileage. At Dead Horse Gulch (mile 19), there was the only major bridge, a remarkably light-looking steel trestle-type bridge 215 ft above the gulch; it has recently been replaced by a short tunnel and quite mundane plate girder bridge. One short tunnel was included in the original route at mileage 16; although only 250 ft long, its construction was a monumental piece of work in view of its precipitous location high on the mountainside and in the absence of modern mining equipment.

All but the first few miles are well above the tree line so that the jagged, rocky country is forbidding in the extreme. Even to see it in summer makes one wonder how the thousands who climbed the pass, many in winter, ever made it. One can see part of the old trail almost at the summit if one knows where to look for the simple but dramatic marker. 'Log Cabin' is now just that, at an elevation of 2,916 ft, but at one time it was a big and busy town, police headquarters for the pass. Bennett (41 miles) is now the divisional point for the railway, daily trains passing here; it consists of the railway station only and yet in its heyday it had a population of 10,000; truly it is a place of ghosts. For twenty-six miles the line winds around the shore of Lake Bennett to Carcross, this being one of the tributaries of the Yukon River, the boundary between British Columbia and the Yukon being passed at mile 53. At Carcross, there may be seen adjacent to the line a diminutive 0—4—0 named the *Duchess*, built by Baldwin in 1878, and used on the 'Taku Tram', a small rail link between Lakes Tagish and Atlin to serve the early settlement of Atlin, one of the historic locomotives of Canada, even though so remote. From Carcross the early travellers continued their hazardous journey by water but the railway cuts directly across to Whitehorse, a pleasant, actively developing town on the Yukon River proper, on the Alaska Highway, and fortunate in having a fine airport.

The Klondike gold rush collapsed and the small Klondike Mine & Municipal Railway was abandoned but the little White Pass railway continued to provide a link between the Yukon and the outside world through Skagway. It had very limited traffic, although tourist passenger traffic was being steadily developed. It was taken over by the US Army during the years of the second world war when it performed yeoman service, as many as seventeen trains a day being operated, despite all difficulties. At the end of the war, maintenance was lamentably behind; the future was in doubt. But its English connections saved the day, a financial reorganisation being carried through by N. D'Arcy in association with Hambros Bank. The company then newly formed has never looked back, and twenty-two million dollars have been spent since then on rehabilitation. In association with the freight that has become available from new mines in the Yukon, with more in prospect, not only has the White Pass line become an active and profitable railway but it has developed into one of the finest examples of a fully integrated transport service.

The railhead is still at Whitehorse but the company operates an efficient trucking business all over the Yukon, feeding into (and from) rail at Whitehorse. The 4-in pipeline laid during the war parallel to the line is the main oil supply line for the territory and a profitable company enterprise. And the outgoing freight to Vancouver is moved in containers on two fine new 6,000 ton special container vessels, their predecessor (the

Clifford J. Rogers, built in 1955) having been the first container ship in the world, just as this small isolated railway pioneered the use of containers for rail-ship transport. At Skagway is a new storage shed for 100,000 tons of the lead-zinc concentrate that is now being brought out of the Yukon at a rate of 1,000 tons a day for direct shipment to Japan and West Germany. It is loaded at the mine into special metal containers that are hauled by truck to railhead and there lifted directly onto specially designed flat-cars for the journey 'down-hill' to the port where they are automatically unloaded.

Thousand-ton ore trains are now hauled by three of the newer diesel locomotives that the WPYR line owns, each developing 1,200 hp, constructed in Canada. They followed the first mainline diesels purchased in 1955, of 800 hp capacity and specially designed (as all WPYR diesels must be) for the unusual climatic conditions in which they have to operate. Snowfall may amount to as much as 426 inches (yes; over 35 ft) at the crest of the line, temperatures going regularly as low as 60°C below zero. Part of the rehabilitation programme has naturally been a complete reballasting of the track and the relaying of rails with 85-lb rail (previous standards having been first 48-lb and then 72), all this work being done by contract. A daily passenger train operates each way. During summer months cruise boats are met on the wharf at Skagway on their early morning arrival by a passenger special that takes its load of tourists up to Bennett (where a splendid luncheon is served, country style) and then back down to Skagway for late afternoon arrival. This is slow travelling, inevitably, but it is on record that in the dark of mid-winter in February 1971, when the weather was so bad that the nearest doctor could not fly into Skagway, a one-car special was operated from Skagway to Whitehorse, up that Big Hill, in 4 hours and 25 minutes, including the necessary long stop at Bennett, in order to take a young girl to the Whitehorse hospital. The great days of Canadian railroading have not yet entirely disappeared.

CHAPTER 15

Railways and Cities: 1971

The new terminal yards of the PGER at North Vancouver and the transhipment berths of the WPYR for their containers have combined with other factors to increase the importance of rail connections between Vancouver and the north side of Burrard Inlet, its fine harbour. In 1969 there was put into use by CNR a new tunnel beneath Capital Hill, Vancouver, connecting their main line just to the east of the city boundary with a new bridge across the Second Narrows of the harbour, giving direct access to North Vancouver and greatly improving rail movements generally, CPR having running rights also on the new line. This is one of the major rail improvements effected in the late sixties in the cities of Canada. Little change has been made generally on the main lines between cities, apart from continuing upgrading of track and signalling facilities, most of recent changes—for better or for worse—having been in and around major cities.

A brief glance may therefore be taken at these changes, in conclusion, starting on the west coast and moving eastward. A new deep-water port has been developed to the south of Vancouver to accommodate large bulk freighters coming from Japan to load up with Canadian coal. Rail service to this new facility has necessitated some rearrangement of lines; as the activity at Robert's Bank (as the new port is known) increases, further changes will be necessary. The large Vancouver passenger terminal used by the CPR for well over half a century is disappearing, to be hidden beneath the towering buildings of a great waterfront development in which the

CP real estate subsidiary company (Marathon Realty) has a leading interest.

The same pattern is found in Calgary, the important divisional point on the CPR before trains enter the mountains. Here the traditional passenger station has disappeared from sight, being now accommodated in the basement of another huge building complex, crowned by a massive concrete tower with a revolving restaurant at its top, yet another joint venture of the Marathon company. On the other hand, outside Calgary a new automated humpyard has been constructed by the CPR at Alyth, which is one of the largest and most efficient in North America. CNR has itself carried out some similar schemes, the long established passenger station in the centre of Saskatoon, on its main line across Saskatchewan, having been removed completely, now replaced by a great office building complex, a new station having been constructed (at a more convenient operating point) four miles away from the city's centre. The fine railway hotels in prairie cities continue their good service, as does the Hotel Vancouver, but the justly famous Royal Alexandra Hotel of the CPR in Winnipeg has been sold to other interests, indicative of the changing passenger picture as far as the CPR is concerned.

Canada's most magnificent railway station is undoubtedly Toronto's Union Station, opened on 6 August 1927 as a part of a massive waterfront redevelopment of rail tracks, all being raised on to a large embankment with concrete bridges so as to give road access to harbour-front property. The great hall of this fine terminal is an architectural masterpiece; it serves well its intended purpose, planning of the twenties having proved adequate even for the tremendous crowds of the war years. (It was said that one gentleman, amid the tugging and pushing of the worst of the pre-Christmas wartime crowds, lost his trousers and was unable to recover them since nobody could bend down, so closely packed were the people.) As this book goes to press, this splendid terminal is also in danger of being swallowed up by the inevitable real estate development (railways again having an interest) but local groups are making valiant efforts to have at least the great hall maintained, for reasons that can be imagined by a glance at the picture on p 144.

Originally, redevelopment plans called for a major new transportation terminal at this location, this concept being in keeping with the efforts that have been made in Toronto to provide adequate rapid transit facilities. The Government of Ontario, through its Department of Transportation and Communications (incorporating the former Department of Highways), is administering and subsidising an imaginative use of the lake-shore tracks of CNR. A fleet of diesel-hauled, and diesel-powered, commuter trains has been provided by the province, the service being operated on convenient schedules by CNR from Pickering, twenty-two miles to the east, through Union Station, to Oakville, twenty-one miles to the west. Bus services, also under contract to the province but operated by Gray Line Coach Lines Ltd and co-ordinated with train schedules, extend the service to points about forty miles east and west, and to Barrie, fifty miles to the north of Union Station. The 'GO-Trains', as the service is popularly known, have proved popular, and the experiment is being watched with keen interest since, if successful, it will mark a significant return to the use of the rails.

Equally significant was the decision right at the end of the second world war by the Toronto Transportation Commission to embark on the construction of Canada's first subway rail system. Starting at Union Station, and running north beneath the main artery of the central city, the first section, only four miles long, was opened in 1955. It is not too much to say that it revolutionised down-town Toronto traffic; extensions have been continually added so that this most efficient electrically-operated system now has about twenty-five route miles in operation. It has rightly attracted the attention of transit authorities from around the world. Other Toronto developments have been less spectacular. Both major railways have improved their freight-handling facilities by new city-avoiding lines and new sorting yards. And CPR still operates its magnificent

Royal York Hotel, with its post-war enlargement still the largest hotel in the Commonwealth and most conveniently located directly adjacent to Union Station.

Montreal also has a new subway system, but very different from that in Toronto. It was opened in 1966, its design being modelled after the Paris Metro with its narrower tunnels and smaller cars, the use of rubber-type wheels being its most novel feature. Some initial difficulties were experienced in the first summer with equipment operation, but these have now been overcome and the system is greatly aiding traffic problems in Montreal which, unlike Toronto, has given up all its electric streetcars, now relying entirely on its municipal bus service and the 'Metro'. In addition, however, Montreal still has its regular commuter trains on both CNR and CPR. CPR extended its lines west of Montreal to Pointe Fortune on the Ottawa River, almost fifty miles from Windsor Street Station, as early as 1891, as a so-called 'suburban line'; as a spur off the new main line to Ottawa, it lasted until 1935. Suburban service was later cut back to start at Rigaud (on the new line) forty miles out from Montreal; this excellent and convenient service continues today. From the days of the GTR until 1961 there was a competing commuter service on the parallel lines from the bridges over the outfall of the Ottawa River into the St Lawrence into the city, but with the rearrangement of the CNR main line this second service was given up. The rearrangement followed the closing of the old Bonaventure Station and the concentration of all CNR trains into Montreal in the splendid new Central Station, an integral part of another great building complex including the Queen Elizabeth Hotel of CNR. From this station there continues to operate the electric suburban service of CN to the northern part of the island of Montreal and beyond. Much study has been given to possible extensions of this service so that more advantageous use might be made of the Mount Royal tunnel (see p 115).

New hump yards for freight-train marshalling have been built by both railways to the west of the city; they have permitted the abandonment of older yards and associated tracks so that rail rearrangements around Montreal still continue to a minor degree. The future of the great Windsor Street Station complex of Canadian Pacific now appears to be in doubt although the excellent approach tracks from the west still exist, serving the two suburban stations of Montreal West and Westmount. All of the terminal tracks in the station have been removed, however, giving this world-famous passenger terminus a forlorn appearance; new platforms have been installed outside. Although no formal notice had been issued by the end of 1971, there are indications that the great building, offices and all, is to be replaced by a modern building complex. Again, local groups are active in attempting to have at least part of this famous building preserved as a quite different sort of architectural heritage from Union Station, Toronto, Windsor Street being notable rather because of its many associations with the life of Canada.

Of the eastern 'triangle' of cities, Ottawa has already lost its Union Station, another splendid piece of architecture, its great hall having been regarded by many as one of the finest examples of interior architectural design in the country. It was also probably one of the most conveniently located of any passenger terminal in North America—but a few hundred yards from the Parliament Buildings of Canada, and so from governmental offices, and connected with the CNR's splendid Chateau Laurier Hotel by a short underground passage. But planners, imbued with the importance of the automobile, decreed that it should go and changed it was, to an inconvenient modern structure on the outskirts of the city at a cost exceeding $30 million. Old rail tracks were torn up just as the civic authorities were first talking seriously about Ottawa's coming need for a rapid transit system. The chaotic track arrangements of both railways in and around Ottawa demanded some drastic revision, especially as the Government of Canada through its National Capital Commission is gradually converting the city to an urban centre truly worthy of being the nation's capital. But there are some, including the writer, who still regard the move of the Ottawa Union Station as a dubious solution if they are correct in thinking that railway passenger traffic is not going to disappear—and CNR are doing their best to see that it does not—and if Ottawa, as seems certain, will soon need a rapid-transit rail system with access to the downtown area. All that can now be said is that the main station building has not been demolished; it was converted, also at great expense, into a governmental conference centre and so 'the glory that has departed' can still be imagined by those who sit at its conference tables.

In the Maritime Provinces to the east, there are changes but none of such import as those in the major cities. Improvements are being made at Moncton, CNR at last building there a CN hotel which will be a boon to this 'hub of the Maritimes' that is also so vital a junction and supply point for all CNR eastern services. CPR have stopped using the small Union Station in Saint John, because of new docking facilities in West Saint John for their steamer service from Digby. Although small by comparison with others to the west, the Saint John station was also conveniently located to serve the downtown area. In Halifax, the big change was made many years ago, starting even before the first world war when a decision was made to build a new rail terminal and hotel at the ocean end of the peninsula on which the city is located. Since valuable industrial property impeded access to the new site beyond existing lines along the waterfront, it was recommended that an entirely new approach be made by encircling the city, even though this meant the excavation of a huge two-mile-long deep rock cutting right through valuable residential property. One can still hear this described as one of the great mistakes made in the history of Canadian civil engineering, but the decision was made, the cutting was excavated, new wharves were built and a well-integrated and splendidly equipped marine-rail terminal was developed, dominated by the Nova Scotia Hotel, enlarged during the sixties. This is the terminal that served so efficiently throughout the second world war and to which due tribute was paid on p 173.

These then, are the Canadian railways of today, still serving well the vast land and its people. CNR account for just over 52 per cent of the total trackage in use, the CPR (CP Rail) almost 37 per cent. The remaining 11 per cent is made up by twenty-four independent lines, the more important of which have been mentioned. Together the QNSLR, PGER, ONR, ACR account for about 7 per cent. About 1 per cent is contributed by the Chesapeake & Ohio Railway with its line through south-western Ontario (the former Pere Marquette Railway). Correspondingly, both CNR and CPR own subsidiary companies in the United States. Canadian National recently formed a new company, the Grand Trunk Corporation, to oversee the administration of its three US subsidiaries—the GTWR with headquarters in Detroit (946 miles), the CVR with 366 miles of track in five of the United States and in Quebec, and the Duluth, Winnipeg & Pacific (one of the old romantic names still persisting) operating 168 miles in central Minnesota, providing connections with western Canada. CPR lines in the United States now total 5,498 miles but no changes in administration have recently been made.

CHAPTER 16

What a Visitor can See

Is there much for a visitor from Europe, interested in railways, to see in Canada? A great deal, despite the dispiriting reports that necessarily have to be given if the same question is asked about the United States of America. Excellent daily train services are available in Canada from coast to coast; many excellent branch-line trains still provide interesting travel. There are exciting developments to see in new forms of civic transport. And although the shrill sound of the whistles of steam locomotives cannot now be heard, nor the thrills experienced of travelling behind one of the massive CPR oil-burning 2—10—4s up the great hill from Field to Hector, there are modern equivalents if the visitor will only accept the inevitability of diesel haulage. Fine examples of the greatest of the steam locomotives that once served Canada so well are to be seen in many parts of the country, most notably near Montreal where today there is one of the finest, if not the finest collection of steam locomotives and other railway memorabilia in North America. As a quick introduction to what can be done in making a railway tour of Canada, a return trip from Atlantic to Pacific will be outlined in the hope that it may prove of assistance, if not of enticement, to those who wish to see what railways still mean to Canada.

One cannot now anticipate, unfortunately, coming across the Atlantic to Canada by boat, this most civilised means of travel having virtually disappeared, apart from very limited accommodation upon a few freighters. Air Canada, however, provides a daily service from England to Halifax where the

216

tour may well start, all mainline passenger rail service on the Newfoundland Railway having been suspended in favour of buses in which no interest need be shown. After recuperating from the long flight in the Nova Scotian Hotel (CN, a good introduction to Canadian railway hotels), it is but a step along a corridor to Union Station from which two routes to Montreal may be followed. If time permits, a DAR diesel railcar (RDC from now on) can be taken at 1100 hr and a pleasant run taken down the Annapolis valley to Digby Wharf, reached at 1520 hr. After a short wait, the *Princess of Acadia* will be boarded for the fifty-mile run across the Bay of Fundy, from 1715 to 2000 hr, with just time to board the Atlantic Limited, a splendidly equipped train of the CPR, using the short line across Maine and reaching Montreal at 0900 hr next morning. The journey will include a first experience of using sleeping berths, or the more convenient roomettes (small cubicles, each with individual folding bed and toilet facilities; excellent unless one suffers from claustrophobia).

Alternatively, one can leave the same station in Halifax at 1130 hr on the Ocean Limited of CNR, to follow the old ICR route all the way to Montreal, reached at 0730 hr next morning. This is also a splendid large train making many interesting stops—at Truro where through cars from Sydney, Cape Breton, will be attached, Moncton with its many railroad facilities, Newcastle, Bathurst, Campbellton (all important industrial towns) and Matapedia Junction at 2035 hr. If the journey is in summer, it will still be light enough to see the small Gaspé line branch train which has brought its through coaches to be attached to The Ocean (picture, p 107); in mid-summer it will be possible also still to see something of the beauty of the Matapedia valley before turning in for the night and a good sleep along the level track running for 250 miles along the flat St Lawrence plain.

There is much to see in Montreal in addition to the city itself and the beauty of its great natural park on Mount Royal. The 'Metro' should be seen and sampled. Central Station itself is worth a good look since it is today almost the last remaining example in Canada of what busy passenger terminals used to be. A trip on one of the electric trains (CNR) through the Mount Royal Tunnel takes little time but shows another facet of the Montreal railway scene. The quiet elegance of Windsor Street Station (CPR) can be imagined as it was in its great days. If the time can be spared, an RDC can be taken three times a week from outside Windsor Street Station up into the Laurentian Mountains, even though the current schedule involves spending a short night at Mont Laurier for the early morning return train. In the fall (early October) this can be a scenically lovely journey and it is the last remaining service of its kind.

A day should be given to going up to the nation's capital city, Ottawa, by the 0810 hr CNR train from Central Station. Despite the slow exit from Montreal, the stop at Dorval for Montreal airport, and single-line working, arrival at Ottawa is at 1009 hr, in effect two hours for the 115.5 mile journey, an example of what Canadian railways can still do. There is a choice of return trains and much to see in Ottawa, the Parliament Building first but with plenty of time left for the National Museum of Science and Technology, housed in a temporary building but including a fine collection of steam locomotives and miscellaneous railway rolling stock, with the maintenance of some of which local members of the Canadian Railroad Historical Association assist.

This active group of railway enthusiasts, with its headquarters in Montreal, has developed its own railway museum at Saint-Constant, a convenient site from the railway point of view to the south of Montreal. Now equipped with two large train sheds, each full of locomotives, it has other equipment standing on outer lines and a complete example of a typical rural railway station. Plans for the future include a running track for locomotives in steam. A recent acquisition was a replica, made in Japan, of the *John Molson* (p 22). Not only are there examples here of most of the well-known Canadian classes, including one of the CPR 2—10—4s, but a blue-liveried Gresley Pacific, *Dominion of Canada*, will be found as well as a Brighton Terrier and examples of French locomotive practice. The Canadian Railway Museum is a must. (Picture, p 72.)

Instead of taking one of the two transcontinental trains in Montreal, the late-afternoon train to Toronto should be boarded at Central Station. The 'Rapido' service is but one evidence of the efforts CNR have been making to improve still further their Montreal-Toronto service. Experiments with a 'Turbo-train' have been disappointing, but this standard diesel-hauled and splendidly equipped train is scheduled to do the 335 miles including two published stops, outside Montreal and Toronto, in one minute under five hours, rather than the six hours of the best steam service. It has the advantage of a fine double track all the way; slows that are almost stops are made at two points to change crews. Few travellers can use this service without being impressed by its excellence and convenience, from down-town to down-town instead of between the maelstroms of busy airports far out from city centres. A stay at the Royal York Hotel in Toronto (CPR) will complete the pleasure of this transfer from Canada's metropolis to its 'Queen City'.

A good ride on the Toronto Subway will be a first priority, with a similar ride on a 'GO-train' as a second; the great potential that these two systems provide for the future of urban transport will be obvious. CNR operates an extensive series of diesel-hauled trains to the busy cities of south-western Ontario, as far as Sarnia and Windsor, but CPR has only one daily RDC (a 'Dayliner') to Windsor. The same type of comfortable but limited service must be used on CNR for a visit to Niagara Falls, another mandatory day for the new visitor to Canada. Going north, one must leave Union Station at 2000 hr on the Northland if time permits of a visit to the Ontario Northland Railway, North Bay being reached at 0120 hr, Cochrane at 0750 hr when the Polar Bear Express to Moosonee can be taken still further north by devoted rail travellers. The only way of getting to Sault Ste Marie, now that through sleeping cars are no longer operated by CPR, is to take The

Canadian leaving Union Station at 1715 hr, detraining at Sudbury at the distressing hour of 2320 hr, there boarding an RDC which sets off into the night at 0015 hr, arriving at The Sault at the uncivilised hour of 0400. Only the hardiest souls would be prepared after this to take the daily northbound train on the Algoma Central but it can be done, leaving The Sault in the summer at 0700 hr and arriving at Hearst at 1745 hr where connection can be made with ONR bus services to Kapuskasing and so to rail services back to Toronto.

After such of these diversions as can be enjoyed, the main journey will also start at Union Station when The Canadian is boarded with a berth booked to Vancouver. A first walk through this quite beautiful train will put out of mind all dismal thoughts about the passenger services that have gone, never to return, for here is rail travelling at its very best, the atmosphere of the dining car, especially at dinner, being something long to be remembered. At Sudbury, the main transcontinental train from Montreal (Train No 1) will be joined, the Toronto section making it a vast train (sometimes up to twenty-two cars) which then starts on its journey to the west at thirty minutes after midnight. White River, allegedly the coldest spot in Canada, or at least in eastern Canada, will be reached at 0805 hr and Lake Superior first seen at Heron Bay at 0925 hr. Then comes the winding and quite fascinating journey along the shore of the great lake, all the more impressive when one remembers the human labour that went into all the rock excavation (and all other work, too) that is so very evident.

Thunder Bay (the new name for the combined cities of Fort William and Port Arthur) is reached at 1440 hr so that the evening hours enable something to be seen of the real, original 'bush country' of the Precambrian Shield. Winnipeg will be reached at·2210 hr, time having now changed from Eastern to Central with a remembrance of Sir Sandford Fleming. Breakfast will be taken as Saskatchewan is left, time now being Mountain—one hour back, with the surprisingly rolling prairie country providing interesting scenery all the way to Calgary, arrival here being at 1305 hr. Then starts the truly fascinating part of the journey, well described in the fine CPR brochure available on the train—Banff and Lake Louise being tempting brief stops before the big climb up to Hector, followed by the even steeper descent to Field through the spiral tunnels. On summer evenings the second great climb up from Beavermouth to the Connaught Tunnel can also be enjoyed, but nightfall will cut out the further pleasures of seeing the remainder of the mountains since the last breakfast will be taken as the great train makes it way across the flat land of the lower Fraser Valley prior to arrival at Vancouver at 1010 hr.

There is still more of Canada to the west but other modes of transport must now be used—an excellent bus service from Vancouver that has a priority place on the singularly efficient B.C. government ferry service that has now almost completely replaced the famous CP Vancouver—Vancouver Island steamers. The bus stops immediately behind the famous Empress Hotel, 'afternoon tea at the Empress' (expensive though it now is) being a fitting climax to this journey from coast to coast, just under 4,000 miles from Halifax. Victoria is a city to be enjoyed at leisure but return to Vancouver should be made by bus to Duncan, close to which can be seen the Cowichan Valley Forest Museum and Railway, a fine collection of logging locomotives (one being usually at work in the summer), then by a further bus journey to Nanaimo where the last remaining CP ferry service can be taken across to Vancouver.

A day trip to Lillooet can then be taken on a PGER RDC with the enjoyment of more superb mountain scenery. Even this will pale if time can be found to spend most of a week in taking the Inland Passage cruise up the west coast as far as Skagway in Alaska, if at all possible on the CNR *Prince George*, one of the finest small ships in which the writer has ever sailed. The cruise itself must be one of the most beautiful in the world but all railway travellers get a special bonus at Skagway in the day trip on the White Pass and Yukon Route up to Bennett, the never-to-be-forgotten all-you-can-eat railway luncheon at the railway station, and the slow descent to the sea again.

Many passengers will always be seen with their backs to the scenery or their eyes closed tight so that they cannot see the precipitous drops to the valley floor below from the train in which they ride.

On the cruise south again to Vancouver, the ship can be left—doubtless with regret—at Prince Rupert and the long return journey to the east started on the daily train that leaves at 1100 hr for yet another lovely run through magnificent mountain scenery all day. Prince George, with its connection to the PGER, gives an alternative way back to Vancouver, and is reached at 2320 hr. A night will therefore be spent in the CNR train before it connects up with the Supercontinental from Vancouver at 0759 hr the next morning. Jasper can be commended for a stay. As the journey continues the contrast with the CPR line gives added interest to the journey, even though it is not comparable either in operating problems (having nothing like the two big climbs of the CP) or in scenery. Edmonton is the first main stop, at 1430 hr; Saskatoon comes at 2205 hr, with another night abed before Winnipeg is reached at 0910 hr next day. If a stop-over is made here, the old *Countess of Dufferin* can be inspected, possibly a run made on the 'Prairie Dog Central Railroad', a fine effort of enthusiasts using a 16-mile disused CNR line, and, for those historically inclined, a boat trip lasting several days up to Norway House, famous Hudson's Bay post, at the north end of Lake Winnipeg. The Hudson's Bay Company, and its stalwart men, will be much in mind as the 1,355-mile journey east to Montreal is made, through seemingly endless forest and lake country, the country through which all the early travellers had to make their way by canoe.

Oba, in the wilds of northern Ontario, will be passed in the night so that there will be no chance of seeing the crossing connection with the ACR. The Toronto and Montreal sections are divided at Capreol, an interesting operation to watch during the brief constitutional that is now possible at longer stops such as this, prior to a good breakfast. One of the disadvantages of diesel haulage is the elimination of most of the divisional point walks for athletic passengers! North Bay will be seen in mid-morning with some evidence of the ONR, and then follows the run down the great valley of the Ottawa River, with occasional glimpses of the river and two crossings, the second of which is very close to the old horse portage railway mentioned on page 27. The right-of-way can still be found, with a lot of searching, in the bush that has long since overgrown it. A stop in Ottawa's modernistic new station in mid-afternoon and then the final run to Montreal, reached at 1745 hr, after a total journey, from Halifax and not counting any side trips, of about 8,000 miles.

CHAPTER 17

L'Envoi

It is but a little more than one hundred years ago that the last official Hudson's Bay Company's canoe journey was made up the Ottawa and on to the west, the great river followed at the end of the rail journey back from the west having been for more than two centuries the gateway to the continent. What changes those hundred years have seen— the whole of Canada surveyed from the air, much of it visited on foot, great cities developed along its southern boundary and a network of railways binding it together from coast to coast. What the next hundred years will bring no man can tell, so rapid and complex has been the industrial and social growth of the country during the last few decades. But if a look ahead as far as the end of the present century is taken, then it is possible to hazard a general prediction as to the place that railways will continue to occupy in the life of the 'Dominion of the North', as Canada has so happily been described.

So vital a part does rail transport play in all the major sectors of the economy—in carrying products of the mines, of the great pulp and paper plants, in serving industrial plants from coast to coast with their supplies and taking away their products, and in transporting the annual movements of grain and the products of the forests—that there should be little basic change in this part of Canadian railroading in the next three decades. Despite great increases in volume, it is improbable that any major change will be made to the essentially single-track character of all Canadian railways. With increased efficiency of operation, and with the experience of the war years to show what can be done on a single-track system, there is little doubt that the railways of Canada will be able to provide the freight services that will be needed to an increasing degree by Canadian industry.

The operation of containers and of unit-trains is already well established. The latter are being used for the transport of potash and sulphur from the prairies to the west coast; recently CNR operated its first oil unit-train from a refinery in Montreal to a large Ontario power station. It has been for the transport of coal, from the coal mines of Alberta and B.C., to the new deep-water port near Vancouver, that the most extensive use of these modern transportation units has yet been seen. CPR are now operating a fleet of 100-car coal trains right through the mountains to the west coast, each train hauled by ten large diesel units up the big hill, spaced throughout the train but all radio-controlled from one engine. Looking even beyond this, CPR engineers have been in Norway to observe special tests of a 3,000 hp Swedish electric locomotive on the Oslo-Bergen line under winter conditions. Electrification of lines through the western Canadian mountains has long been discussed; increased freight loads may yet make it an economic proposition. It has been suggested that shipments of Canadian coal to Japan might reach sixty million tons a year by the 1980s, in contrast to the ten million tons of the sixties, probably rising to forty million tons by the mid-seventies. Handling these impressive amounts over the existing lines through the mountains will tax the resources of Canadian railways but it is certain that they will be able to meet this challenge.

The probable increase in the volume of freight to be carried will make even more difficult than at present the operation of long-distance passenger trains. The future of the Canadian transcontinental services is under critical review by the Canadian Transport Commission. It seems probable, and is greatly to be hoped, that one through train from Montreal-Toronto to Vancouver will continue in operation even though it may not be a daily service other than during summer months; it may also be some form of joint operation between CPR and CNR.

Canadian National may be expected to continue its active development of inter-city services, with the Montreal to Toronto route the real testing ground for the whole future of rail passenger transport in Canada. Unfortunately, CPR must be written-off in any forecasting of future passenger services, the company having already shown publicly its desire to become a freight-only line, in association with its now varied financial interests.

An experimental rail link from the city of Montreal to its new international airport will show what possibilities exist for this new type of urban rail service. This will be a part of the almost certain development of new rapid transit systems in a number of major Canadian cities, some initial studies being already in progress. The experience gained in both Montreal and Toronto will be helpful in these further developments. Of special significance was the action of the Ontario Government in 1971 in halting construction of a multi-million dollar major expressway already well started, planned to run into downtown Toronto. The decision was warmly greeted by the majority of citizens, even though violent objections were naturally raised in those quarters that are wedded to still further encroachments of the private automobile. It is clear that public transit, and specifically rail transit, is going to be well used in the further development of Toronto.

It will be in the north of Canada that the most exciting developments are to be expected, especially if more mines are discovered of such value that rail links can be built to them. Extension of the PGER into the Yukon Territory in association with the Government of Canada, is at least a possibility. This could well mean the eventual conversion to standard gauge of the WPYR, the extension of which into the Yukon to replace existing road services is yet another possibility. Suggestions have even been made of extending the Pine Point line of CNR up into the Arctic in order to provide for the transport of oil from the Arctic slope to the markets of North America. This might be an ecologically desirable alternative to the pipelines that are generally assumed to be the 'only' means by which the valuable petroleum products already discovered on the Arctic coast will be brought south. It represents another phase of the keen competition that already exists between the railways and pipeline companies. The table on p 186 shows the important place that pipelines already occupy in the Canadian transportation scene. Pipelines already exist in the United States for the transportation of coal, as a slurry; experiments on the use of pipelines for wheat have been conducted.

The future of transportation in Canada is therefore full of challenge. Railways will continue to be a major carrier for many years to come. Their great traditions and century-old record of fine service provide a firm basis for their further development as a vital part of the transportation network of this second largest country in the world.

Appendices

APPENDIX 1

Some Canadian Railway Statistics

Canada is fortunate in having a national statistical agency of outstanding repute. Founded in 1918 to continue work previously done by the Department of Agriculture and other divisions of the government of Canada, it was widely known for over fifty years as the Dominion Bureau of Statistics. 'DBS' were the identifying initials on a long series of useful publications. Its name has been changed to 'Statistics Canada' but its work continues unchanged. Its best known publication is probably the annual *Canada Year Book*, now a volume of over 1,400 pages, a real compendium of factual information about all major aspects of Canadian life. The following tables have been prepared to indicate the main features of Canadian railway development. All figures have come from DBS publications, to the transportation parts of which the tables merely provide an introduction. Readers wishing to obtain more detailed statistical information should address their enquiries to The Director of the Transportation and Public Utilities Division, Statistics Canada, Ottawa, Canada.

Appendix 1

TOTAL MAINLINE MILEAGE

Year	Mileage
1835	0
1840–45	16
1850	66
1855	877
1860	2,065
1865	2,240
1870	2,617
1875	4,804
1880	7,194
1885	10,773
1890	13,151
1895	15,977
1900	17,657
1905	20,487
1910	24,731
1915	34,882
1920	38,845
1925	40,350
1930	42,047
1935	42,916
1940	42,565
1945	42,352
1950	42,979 (a)
1955	43,444
1960	44,029
1965	43,157
1969	43,613

(a) Newfoundland Railway mileage included;

Closure of many branch lines during the last two decades has been compensated, in mileage, by the opening of new lines such as those in the northern parts of Canada.

PRINCIPAL OPERATING STATISTICS

Year	Total Train Miles	Passengers: No	Freight: Tons
1875	17,680,178	5,190,416	5,670,836
1880	22,427,449	6,462,948	9,938,858
1885	31,623,689	9,672,599	14,659,271
1890	41,849,329	12,821,272	20,787,469
1895	40,418,324	12,520,585	21,524,421
1900	42,647,684	17,122,193	35,764,970
1905	65,934,114	25,288,723	50,893,957
1910	85,409,241	35,894,575	74,482,866
1913	113,437,208 (a)	46,230,765	106,992,716
1915	93,218,479	46,322,035	87,204,838
1920	107,053,735	51,318,422	127,429,154
1925	109,289,865	41,458,084	111,251,241
1930	107,620,076	34,698,767	115,229,511
1935	79,452,417	20,031,839	93,374,494
1940	94,282,567	21,969,871	125,167,291
1944	130,140,335 (b)	60,335,950	155,326,332
1945	127,780,196	53,407,845	147,348,566
1950	125,141,312	30,167,145	144,218,319
1955	124,228,545	27,229,962	167,862,156
1960	98,380,182	19,497,233	158,466,368
1965	99,132,185	23,610,374	225,356,167
1969	99,106,175	23,694,748	231,217,882

Notes: (a) Figures for 1913 are included since this was the peak year for traffic prior to the first world war.

(b) Correspondingly, figures for 1944 are given since this was the peak year for traffic up to that time from the start of Canadian railroads; passenger traffic has never been the same since that time but annual freight traffic passed this wartime peak in the early sixties.

The significant decrease in total train miles in relation to volume of freight traffic during the sixties will be noted, an indication of one of the economies of diesel haulage.

232 *Appendix 1*

ROLLING STOCK OF CANADIAN RAILWAYS

Year	Locomotives	Passenger Coaches	Freight Cars
1868	485	684	6,604
1890	1,771	2,018	52,356
1895	2,023	3,148	56,963
1900	2,273	2,634	66,886
1905	2,906	3,130	87,574
1910	4,079	4,320	119,733
1915	5,486	6,326	201,790
1920	6,030	6,557	224,489
1925	5,752	6,839	224,227
1930	5,451	7,346	215,027
1935	4,795	6,669	176,760
1940	4,308	6,267	160,097
1945	4,431	6,211	164,769
1950	4,655	6,338	175,597
1955	4,714	6,574	185,956
1960	3,752	5,119	191,553
1965	3,323	3,638	182,096
1969	3,316	2,942	188,268

Comparison of these figures with those in the preceding table will confirm the economy being introduced by diesel haulage, the decrease in passenger service, and more efficient handling of freight.

THE CHANGE-OVER FROM STEAM TO DIESEL HAULAGE

Year	Locomotives			
	Steam	Diesel	Electric	Total
1947	4,384	54	33	4,451
1948	4,338	148	34	4,520
1949	4,351	246	30	4,627
1950	4,272	350	33	4,665
1951	4,108	574	33	4,715
1952	4,014	763	33	4,810
1953	3,829	956	33	4,818
1954	3,586	1,152	33	4,771
1955	3,225	1,445	33	4,714
1956	2,849	1,895	46	4,790
1957	2,394	2,372	55	4,821
1958	1,960	2,799	64	4,823
1959	1,514	3,155	51	4,720
1960	403	3,308	41	3,752
1961	197	3,309	41	3,547
1962	137	3,320	39	3,496
1963	7	3,347	31	3,385
1964	1	3,281	22	3,304
1965	—	3,301	22	3,323

The end of an era.

CANADIAN ELECTRIC RAILWAYS

Year	Mileage	Train Miles	Passengers
1895	56	560,447	1,751,588
1900	681	30,924,355	118,129,862
1905	793	45,959,101	203,467,217
1910	1,047	65,249,166	360,964,876
1915	1,590	96,964,829	562,302,373
1920	1,699	114,481,406	804,711,333
1925	1,737	119,684,151	725,491,101
1930	1,508	140,014,600	792,701,493
1935	1,268	120,816,349	600,728,313
1940	1,040	128,254,433	691,737,901
1945	1,015	130,365,430	1,043,768,631
1950	662	88,059,060	688,981,995
1955	509	55,650,898	406,877,571

Since most Canadian electric railways were associated with or extensions of urban street-car systems, even the main 'inter-urban' lines serving as local lines within city boundaries, it has always been impossible to separate electric railways proper from electric street-car systems. The above figures therefore include both. After the second world war, all the 'inter-urban' lines quickly disappeared so that, even by 1950, about 60 per cent of the traffic noted in the table was on the Montreal and Toronto street-car systems. Montreal gave up all street-cars in the late fifties but opened its electric subway system in 1966. Toronto retains street-cars on some important routes; it opened the first section of its subway system in 1954. Figures beyond those given in the table would therefore represent, in effect, traffic on these two urban systems, plus the suburban traffic from Central station, Montreal, on the electric trains still operated through the Mount Royal tunnel by CNR.

Appendix 1

DEATHS AND INJURIES ON CANADIAN RAILWAYS

(due to railway operation)

	Killed:		
Year	*Passengers*	*Total*	*Injured*
1875	?	92	289
1880	?	102	807
1885	?	157	684
1890	11	218	838
1895	9	187	658
1900	7	323	1,304
1905	35	468	1,355
1910	62	615	2,139
1915	17	379	4,978
1920	29	393	8,680
1925	5	309	9,248
1930	15	463	11,063
1935	10	351	6,286
1940	5	300	7,215
1945	10	354	14,351
1950	18	317	9,149
1955	1	307	5,254
1960	2	262	1,586
1965	2	229	2,077
1969	4	195	1,852

Note: The great difficulty of accurately defining injuries due to any specific cause is reflected in the variability of the above figures for railway injuries. Some of the older records suggest some changes in reporting but the record of passenger deaths, even at five-year intervals, is a good indication of the generally excellent safety record of Canadian railway operation, despite its essential single-line character.

APPENDIX 2

Abbreviations used in Text

ACR	Algoma Central Railway
AStLR	Atlantic & St Lawrence Railroad
BCR	British Columbia Railway (formerly PGER)
CRHA	Canadian Railroad Historical Association
CLC	Canadian Locomotive Co Ltd, Kingston
CNR	Canadian National Railways
CNOR	Canadian Northern Railway (now CNR)
CPR	Canadian Pacific Railway (now CPRail)
CVR	Central Vermont Railway
DAR	Dominion Atlantic Railway
GTPR	Grand Trunk Pacific Railway (now CNR)
GTR	Grand Trunk Railway (now CNR)
GTWR	Grand Trunk Western Railroad (now CNR)
ICR	Intercolonial Railway (now CNR)
MCR	Michigan Central Railroad
MLCR	Montreal & Champlain Railroad
MLW	Montreal Locomotive Works Ltd
NAR	Northern Alberta Railways
NTR	National Transcontinental Railway (now CNR)
NYCRR	New York Central Rail Road
ONR	Ontario Northland Railway (formerly TNOR)
PGER	Pacific Great Eastern Railway (now BCR)
QMOOR	Quebec, Montreal, Ottawa & Occidental Railway
QNSLR	Quebec North Shore & Labrador Railway
StLAR	St Lawrence & Atlantic Railroad
TNOR	Temiskaming & Northern Ontario Railway (now ONR)
WPYR	White Pass & Yukon Route

235

Suggestions for Further Reading

These notes suggest sources of information supplementary to the two main reference books noted under 'Acknowledgements', most of which were used in the preparation of this book and which may be of interest to those who wish for more information on one or other of the major topics. Since a number of issues of *Canadian Rail* are mentioned, this monthly magazine will be referred to merely as *CR*.

Ch. 1.   The Beginnings: 1836–54

CR No 200, June 1968: 'The Champlain and St Lawrence Railroad; first years of operation' by S. S. Worthen.

CR No 229, Feb. 1971: 'Jason C. Pierce; the Man and the Machine' by J. B. Thompson.

CR No 177, May 1966: 'The Montreal and Lachine Rail Road and its successors' by R. G. Bales.

Can. RR Hist. Assoc., Bulletin No 18 (later *CR*) No 18, Oct. 1954: 'The Last Broad Gauge' (the Carillon & Grenville Railway) by R. R. Brown.

Spanner No 209, Jan. 1955: 'Historic Review of "Bytown and Prescott Railway" as Ottawa Observes Centenary First Railway Service' by O. S. A. Lavallée

CRHA Bulletin No 6, Aug. 1938: 'Railroads of the General Mining Association (Nova Scotia)' by R. R. Brown.

Ch. 2.   The Grand Trunk: 1845–62

Hewson M. B., *The Grand Trunk Railway of Canada*, Toronto 1876.

Ch. 3.   Battle of the Gauges: 1851–80

CR No 141 Feb. 1963: 'The Rise and Fall of the Provincial Gauge' by O. S. A. Lavallée.

The Gazette (Montreal) 23 March 1957: 'The Railway Crash that Shook Canada' by E. A. Collard.

Ch. 4. The Intercolonial: 1858–76

Fleming, Sandford, *The Intercolonial: A History—1832 to 1876*, Montreal 1876.

Penney A. R., 'The Newfoundland Railway—Newfoundland Epic' in *The Book of Newfoundland*, vol 3, pp 473–502, J. Smallwood ed., St John's 1967.

Ch. 5. Surveys for the Transcontinental Railway: 1872–80

Reports of Sandford Fleming are available as official documents but the overall story has been told by Pierre Berton in *The National Dream*, Toronto 1970.

Ch. 6. Building the Canadian Pacific Railway: 1881–86

Berton P.: *The Last Spike*, Toronto 1971, is the companion volume to that noted above, written in graphic style.

Innes H. A.: *History of the Canadian Pacific Railway*, Toronto 1922, now reprinted by David & Charles, 1971.

Gibbon J. M.: *Steel of Empire*, Toronto 1935.

These are but four of the better known of the many books published on this subject. In 1937, Canadian Pacific Railways itself published *Canadian Pacific Facts and Figures*, a 257-page volume that contains useful information not available elsewhere.

Ch. 7. Branch and Other Lines: 1882–1905

Brown R. R.: *The Ice Railway*, a special publication of the C.R.H.A., Montreal 1960.

Railway Magazine (London), vol 110, Feb. 1964: 'Canadian Branch Line Mortalities' by R. F. Legget.

CR No 156, June 1964: 'Ottawa, Arnprior and Parry Sound' by O. S. A. Lavallée.

Ch. 8. Canadian Northern Railway: 1896–1917

Hanna D. B.: *Trains of Recollections*, Toronto 1924, the author having been general manager of the line.

Ch. 10.   Canadian National Railway: 1923–32

Stevens G. R.: *Canadian National Railways*, Toronto, vol 1, 1960; vol 2, 1962.

Marsh D'Arcy: *The Tragedy of Henry Thornton*, Toronto 1935.

Ch. 11.   Canadian Pacific Railway: 1886–1932

Books already listed, other than those by Pierre Berton, deal also with the later history of the CPR. See also:

Vaughan W.: *The Life and Work of Sir William van Horne*, New York 1920.

Ch. 12.   Years of Depression and War: 1932–46

CR No 231, April 1971: 'Canada's Classic Interurbans; the 130-class cars of the Niagara St Catherines and Toronto Railway' by M. P. Murphy.

Canadian National Magazine, Nov. and Dec. 1941: 'How our Central Traffic Control Speeds War Traffic', (information reprinted from *Railway Age*).

Ch. 14.   Lines to the North: 1899–1971

Information obtained from the managements of the five independent lines, with offices at:

Quebec, North Shore and Labrador Railway; Sept Iles, Que;

Ontario Northland Railway: North Bay, Ont.;

Algoma Central Railway: Sault Ste. Marie, Ont.;

Pacific Great Eastern Railway (British Columbia Railways): 1095 West Pender St, Vancouver, B.C.;

White Pass and Yukon Route: 510 West Hastings St, Vancouver, B.C.;

Some idea of the problems of building far northern railways is given by:

Charles J. L.: 'Permafrost Aspects of Hudson Bay Railroad', Proc. American Soc. of Civil Engs., Jour. Soil Mechanics Div., vol 85, No SM6, p 125, Dec. 1959.

Ch. 15.   Railways and Cities: 1971

CR No 179, July–Aug. 1966: 'Ottawa Union Station Closes' by O. S. A. Lavallée.

CR No 221, May 1970: 'Railway Entrances to Vancouver, 1887–1969' by D. E. Cummings.

General
From the extensive literature on Canadian railways, four further titles may usefully be noted:

Keefer T. C.: *Philosophy of Railroads*, Montreal 1850; (a very early publication by a noted pioneer civil engineer).

Skelton O. D.: *The Railway Builders* (Vol 32 of the *Chronicles of Canada*), Toronto 1916

Lovett H. A.: *Canada and the Grand Trunk*, Montreal 1924.

Fournier L. T.: *Railway Nationalization in Canada*, Toronto 1935.

Acknowledgements

The writer of any such concise history of the railways of Canada as this short volume is naturally beholden to the master historians who have laboriously assembed and synthesized the many details of the great story that is herein so briefly told. I am therefore greatly indebted to Dr G. P. de T. Glazebrook whose *A History of Transportation in Canada* (Toronto, 1938; revised edition in 2 vols, Toronto, 1964) presents on a broad canvas the whole political and economic development of railways in Canada up to the mid-thirites; to the late N. Thompson and J. H. Edgar, authors of *Canadian Railway Development* (Toronto, 1933) which gives useful historical information about the building and operation of the railways of Canada up to the early thirties; and finally to the successive editors of *Canadian Rail*. This excellent monthly journal is published by the Canadian Railroad Historical Association (PO Box 22, Station 'B', Montreal, Que) and reached its 250th issue in October of 1972. Specific references to individual issues will be found in *Suggestions for Further Reading*. Many of its articles amplify, and in some cases correct, the information given by Thompson and Edgar. Without the aid of these useful summaries of railway facts, this volume could not have been written. I acknowledge gratefully my indebtedness.

Mr S. S. Worthen, the present editor of *Canadian Rail*, has kindly aided me greatly by a critical reading of the book in draft form; it is the better for his sage and expert advice. Dr Glazebrook, Dr J. H. Jenkins and Dr J. L. McDougal have also been good enough to read the text and to give me the benefit of considered opinions. Other friends who have also helped in different ways, especially with illustrations, include Mr O. S. A. Lavallée (CPR Montreal), Miss R. S.

Gallagher and Mr J. G. Coté (CNR Montreal), Messrs. Stanley Triggs (Curator of the Notman Archives at McGill University, Montreal), J. Caulfield Smith of Oakville and E. H. Q. Smith of Ottawa. Staff members of Statistics Canada and of the Public Archives of Canada, and the General Managers of the five independent 'Lines to the North' were similarly helpful. To all I am grateful.

Despite all this friendly assistance, I am conscious of the shortcomings of this attempt to present such a vast and complex story within the confines set for this series of volumes. I regret the necessary omissions but accept full responsibility for the essential selectivity of material, as I do also for the errors that must undoubtedly still remain. I shall appreciate advice from readers who notice any such inaccuracies. Finally, I must record my indebtedness to Mr T. Stanhope Sprigg, director of David & Charles Ltd, for his invitation to prepare this volume, his interest in its development and his attention to its production. I can but hope that it meets, in some degree, his aspiration and that it will enable readers to glimpse the fascination that the railways of Canada have had for me ever since I made my first train journey in this country, from Halifax to Montreal, now more than forty years ago.

Ottawa,   ROBERT F. LEGGET
May 1972

Index

242

PART TWO: PLACE NAMES

PART THREE: INDEX OF SUBJECTS